BONSAI

A BEGINNER'S GUIDE ON HOW TO CULTIVATE, GROW,
AND TAKE CARE OF BONSAI TREES

KABUTO ARATA

Respective authors own all copyrights not held by the publisher.

The information herein is offered for informational purposes solely, and is universal as so. The presentation of the information is without contract or any type of guarantee assurance.

The trademarks that are used are without any consent, and the publication of the trademark is without permission or backing by the trademark owner. All trademarks and brands within this book are for clarifying purposes only and are owned by the owners themselves, not affiliated with this document.

WHY YOU SHOULD READ THIS BOOK

Are you thinking of decorating your house with bonsai trees? In any case, such miniature trees will be very refreshing to look at. They add beauty to your home and relax your tired body and mind. Placing houseplants in your home can actually benefit you in several ways, aside from adding beauty to your home. For example, did you know that plants can make your breathing easier? Try to remember your earlier science lesson. You have certainly come across the perception of photosynthesis, in which plants absorb carbon dioxide and release oxygen. When breathing, we do the opposite: absorb oxygen and release carbon dioxide. Plants can make your breathing easier. In this context, plants can also purify the air by eliminating their toxins. They can also help solve breathing problems by increasing humidity. Growing this type of plant is a challenging task. When growing houseplants, you need to pay special attention to them. What else do you need if you plan to grow them? Bonsai requires a lot of intelligence, persistence, and discipline. Therefore, you should be really committed if you want to take care of this tree type. If there is insufficient indoor water, air, and sunlight, your plants will suffer. Water your bonsai trees more often than outdoor plants. It would be best if you watered them regularly, but be careful not to pour them over. It's best to ask bonsai experts about the right way to water your bonsai, especially those that are placed indoors. But in general, indoor bonsai trees should be watered more often than outdoor bonsai trees.

Table of Contents

LISTEN TO THE AUDIOBOOK FOR FREE

DID YOU KNOW YOU CAN DOWNLOAD THE AUDIOBOOK VERSION OF THIS BOOK FOR FREE?

- VISIT **BIT.LY/BONSAI-US** FOR AUDIBLE US
- VISIT **BIT.LY/BONSAI-UK** FOR AUDIBLE UK

INTRODUCTION

T HE HISTORY OF THE bonsai tree is indeed long and rich in tradition. Although Japan has most of the earnings against the background of the bonsai tree, historians believe that the first lifestyle that actually practices miniaturized tree growing has come from the Chinese. Numerous historians believe that the bonsai tree was attractive for this ancient culture simply because the potted tree was so gnarled and leaf-free that the potted tree looked more like a medieval animal than a tree. The Japanese part of the bonsai background started sometime during the Kamakura period. The Kamakura period from Japan's records was when Buddhism quickly became more attractive through Asia. The Kamakura period lasted from 1135 to 1333. When Japan adopted the Chinese habit of planting small trees in pots, the history of bonsai was given a completely new face. The Japanese were not content to grow a handful of unusually shaped trees of indefinite species. They wanted their beautiful ornamental trees to be potted too. At first, the tiny gnarled trees were only visible in the gardens of Buddhist temples. Still, as the bonsai tree record developed, the trees gradually appeared in the gardens, which were eventually also tended by aristocrats and kings. At the end of the Kamakura period, growing bonsai was a respected Japanese art. A few centuries after the Kamakura period ended, few experiences within the records in regards to bonsai ₁changed. It was still a symbol of

Japanese culture. It had been spotted frequently in gardens, and some of the aristocrats brought their humble potted trees inside for short periods of energy. During this time, Westerners were given permission to enter Japan. For the first time, travelers could really appreciate the unusual beauty of the bonsai tree. Nowadays, bonsai trees can be observed in houses and gardens around the world.

The word "bonsai" conjures up so many thoughts about many people. Almost a warrior sound, but in reality, the word bonsai implies a miniature tree. Most of us relate bonsai with the Japanese. Apparently, the art of bonsai protection and development, as we know it today, has its origins in China and was referred to as pensai in China. Pensai was used until about 600 BC. The word "bon" consists of two parts: "bonsai" means shell and "sai" means plant, which literally means "shell plant". We strive to ensure that we correctly label bonsai trees when part of the word derivative actually means plants. The art of bonsai started in China more than 1,000 years ago, supposedly during the Han Period, and was originally known as "penjing" or tray planting. The Penjing artist's goal was to recreate a natural landscape in a container with dwarf trees and miniature hills, valleys, rivers, and lakes. Bonsai was inaugurated to the Japanese aristocracy as a symbol of prestige and honor. The Japanese quickly became masters of flourishing these twisted and dwarf trees in containers, and bonsai developed into a highly developed art form, especially in the 17th and 18th centuries. The tradition soon spread to the general population. In the mid-19th century, visitors to Japan brought bonsai to the rest of the world. The third Paris World Exhibition in 1878 and other exhibitions in London,

Vienna, and Paris sparked western interest in bonsai, and until the term of World War II, the art of bonsai became even more popular. Soldiers returned to the US with bonsai trees, and the Japanese-American population then helped teach Americans how to cultivate bonsai. The bonsai exhibitions in Japan also increased international interest in the tradition. The exhibition did not take place for four years during the Second World War. Books about bonsai art were published in English and other languages in the 1950s.

In 1952, bonsai kindergartens and clubs were also becoming increasingly popular outside of Japan. Individuals and groups traveled to Japan to study in Japanese bonsai kindergartens and brought their newly gained expertise back to local clubs. The American Bonsai Association was founded in 1967, and a 1970 World's Fair was held in Osaka in 1970. A great bonsai display was part of this event. Three monthly bonsai magazines were founded in the 1970s: Bonsai Sekai, Satsuki Kenkyu, and Shizen to Bonsai. In 1980, the first World Bonsai Conference was held in Osaka during the Bonsai and Suiseki World's Fair. Suiseki is the Japanese art of stone estimation. These stones often resemble an animal or human figure or landscapes. Today bonsai congresses take place worldwide. Bonsai trees, pots, tools, and garden supplies are not only available in Japan, but also in nurseries worldwide. Bonsai is the art of keeping trees in pots. The art of bonsai actually derives from the Chinese art of penzai and penshing. Bonsai and Penzai are translated as "Tray Plant" or "Tray Cultivation", while Penjing is translated as "Tray Scenery". As the name suggests, Penjing focuses more on landscapes such as mountain rocks, which usually include trees and plants. In the current western world, the word bonsai is used more to describe one of these arts, and basically describes any trees that are kept in a flat tray or pot. The general goal of bonsai is to create a small tree in a pot that looks like an ancient ripe wild tree. The methods include branch and root cutting, branch shaping, reduction of leaf size, and the production of deadwood areas (Jin / Shari).

In Japan, the focus was less on landscapes than on individual trees in pots. This is believed to be due in part to the principles of Zen Buddhism, which emphasized "beauty in the strict economy", but also to the relatively small size of Japan compared to the vast mountainous landscapes of China. This led to a focus on very well-kept, precisely shaped individual trees in pots, as most people would probably think of them today as bonsai. The Japanese enlarged many formal styles for bonsai, and the trees were operated to a much higher degree than their peers in China, which generally look wilder and are often in more colorful and patterned pots. In the 17th and 18th centuries, art was particularly popular with the Japanese elite. It played a role in everyday life, and often a small area of the house was dedicated to the exhibition of bonsai. The western world only lately became conscious of bonsai and began to create it. Several worldwide exhibitions showed bonsai, especially in the Paris World Exposition 1900 and a London exhibition in 1909 when the world began to see these splendid trees for themselves and the enthusiasm spread. The Japanese, and, later, the Chinese evolve nurseries to produce bonsai for the mass export market. This market has increased and continues to grow, although more and more trees have recently been imported from China. Ironically, bonsai started in China, but was adopted and popularized by the Japanese all over the world. Today, the Chinese are taking over the world market for bonsai again.

Bonsai is a stunted tree, plant, or shrub that literally grows in a tray. Indeed, this is the actual dry definition of the infinitely beautiful art of creating a bonsai, an art as sublime and spectacular as painting. Unfortunately, this dry definition does not add to the uniqueness of this art form. In order to build a work of art, there has to be a medium. In the case of bonsai, this basic medium, the stunted plant continues to grow and is full of life. In short, you create a piece of resistance from a living being full of vitality! The art of bonsai is ancient and comes from the Land of the Rising

Sun. It is an oriental specialty and a horticultural art form that has taken the whole world by storm and made a frenzy. To create a bonsai, you first need to select specific types and shapes of bonsai, prune the plant and train in the shape you want to call it bonsai. Any damn potted plant is not a bonsai. Bonsai are miniature forms of the same giant trees that grow on the ground. The only dissimilarity is that they are tiny and kept small by carefully controlling the growing conditions of the plant. In short, you intercept the natural growth process of the plant and manipulate nature to produce this stunted masterpiece. You must heartlessly cut off all types of undesirable growth, that is, unwanted branches, and keep only the branches that will later contribute to the overall design of the stunted horticulture. In a pot or bowl, you need to restrict the roots and cut the roots off at regular intervals. Bonsai must remain true to nature, the shape and design of the plant species must be identical to the original. At the same time, one can also indulge in exaggeration or stylization. Bonsai can survive hundreds of years, and the older a bonsai is, the more valuable it is. Like normal trees, bonsai is subject to seasonal and annual changes, and over the decades, they bloom in their true beauty. However, you need to prune them, cut them, and train them throughout their lifespan.

Bonsai trees are made from normal trees or shrubs. A bonsai should be a perfect miniature of the same tree that has grown up in its natural habitat. Basically, trees get as big as possible when left to their own devices. As a bonsai artist, you put a selected tree in the shade and prevent it from accelerating towards the sky. Why do that? Well, you can't have a 40-foot elm tree on the table at a dinner party, can you? In order for a plant or tree to be considered bonsai, the plant must be miniaturized successfully. This is achieved by pruning and limiting root growth. If you prune a bonsai tree during each growing season, new shoots can thrive under your control. With careful care, the tree must not assume its natural shape. This keeps the tree at a very low height but promotes trunk strength and balanced, symmetrical leaf cushions. This requires planning, and you need to develop a vision for your tree. The overall size of a bonsai can vary considerably and they can get quite old, even as old as humans! Bonsai trees have a reputation for old age, but the plant does not have to reach a certain age to be considered bonsai. The mighty bonsai pine can live for thousands of years! Let us make one thing clear, a bonsai is an art form. Depending on the processing, a 10-year-old specimen can look as strong as a 100-year-old! The wonderful and exciting thing about bonsai is that a bonsai lives differently than a painting or a sculpture. It breathes and grows. It is a work of art that is always going on. As an artist, the tree is your theme, and you paint a picture with every twist and turn of a branch. To achieve certain shapes, wiring is required to bring each branch of a tree into the positions you want. There is a special method for wiring, but it is quite easy to learn.

The art form is cultural, spiritual, and has an extensive

history. In Chinese culture, bonsai was an art form for almighty figures. Artists are said to have had special powers. Today there is a feeling of spirituality known as Zen Bonsai. You literally have to experience the satisfaction of training dwarf trees and seeing them grow into proud and mystical works of art. It's easy, of course, with the right advice and knowledge. A word of warning! Make sure that when you buy a bonsai that it is a real bonsai. Anyone can plant small shrubs in a pot, but a real bonsai is identified by type, age, and appearance. Don't just buy a shrub in a pot! Buy in a local kindergarten or online. There are many myths associated with bonsai. This not only confuses incipient enthusiasts but also gives the pastime an imperfect name. A bonsai is not a genetically outclassed plant and is in no way kept small by cruelty.

Bonsai techniques are no more cruel than other horticultural efforts. With an adequate supply of water, air, light, and nutrients, a properly cared for bonsai should survive a tree of the same species at full size. One myth is that bonsai are only a few centimeters tall. This is not wholly true, although bonsai are small compared to their tall, life-size brothers. Most of them are over 20 centimeters tall and up to 1 to 1.2 meters high.

Contrary to what most people believe, bonsai trees are not natural dwarf trees, but normal trees that are kept short by continuous maintenance, pruning and repotting. With this in mind, people interested in bonsai art have recognized the need to learn the basics of bonsai. Otherwise, the trees cannot be kept alive and well cared for. Thanks to experts who offer bonsai courses, many people have learned the art and even perfected it. Bonsai trees are unique and beautiful plants, so you should try to acquire all the skills required to maintain these plants as such. The art of bonsai borders on the regulation of sunlight, fertilizer, pruning, and water. If you learn how to deal with these four things, you can grow good trees and maintain their health. However, this skill takes a considerable amount of time and effort and also requires some research, but can be somewhat facilitated by attending bonsai courses. Learning bonsai skills also requires a lot of practice. For this reason, most people start with native tree species to minimize the costs that mistakes can incur.

Patience in bonsai growing is a virtue that is very impressed in bonsai lessons. Any bonsai professional will tell you that it is the strength you need to maintain healthy and beautiful bonsai trees. Understanding the needs of such trees and providing the best environment and care for healthy growth takes time. It is only a person with this virtue who can actually be successful in bonsai art. Carefully maintained bonsai trees can be over a hundred years old and, as such, bring in thousands of dollars should they be sold. To speed up bonsai lessons, some professionals encourage students to practice with herbs and chrysanthemums. These perennial plants grow much faster and can help you to continuously put the skills and knowledge acquired in class into practice. Herbs are preferred because they reach a practical size in just one season, and you can learn more in less time. Bonsai course participants are also always encouraged to enjoy learning as much as possible to prevent the courses from becoming monotonous sessions. It is also good to accept mistakes and learn from them. This will help you deal more perfectly with oriental bonsai trees from Japan, China, and other Asian countries. The skills and virtues that you acquire in learning bonsai art can also help you solve life's problems from a much better perspective.

TYPES OF BONSAI TREES

SOME PEOPLE BELIEVE THAT bonsai trees are a specific species, but all types of plants, shrubs, or trees can be developed using bonsai growing techniques. Bonsai is an oriental art form that miniaturizes all types, but trees and shrubs are the most popular. Different types of bonsai trees can include elms, oaks, maples and cedars or pines, and juniper trees are interesting when miniaturized. Bonsai tree cultivation began as a Japanese art, but spread to the Chinese, making these two countries one of the largest exporters of bonsai soil, planters, and tools. There really aren't many secrets to learn as growing different types of bonsai trees has become popular around the world. The key is pruning properly, training branches, and of course, limiting roots to miniaturize each type. You can choose fruit trees like a lemon tree or a flowering shrub-like an azalea. After ripening, they still produce flowers and fruits, but if you use these growing techniques properly, they will be small in size. Some people choose to build a bonsai orange tree or a grapefruit tree from seeds of their fruits bought in the store. Because a bonsai tree can grow for 100 years, these trees can bloom, bear fruit, and fallen seeds can produce offspring from your flowering or fruiting bonsai tree. It is not uncommon for gingko, fichus, jade, mimosa, or other types of ornamental plants and oriental miniature species to be used in the bonsai garden. Since this artistically expressive practice of growing and training miniature trees has been practiced in Asian cultures for centuries, it is not uncommon to find Chinese elms, Japanese maple trees, or bamboo.

Different types of bonsai trees can include popular shrubs such as boxwood, yew, and even lilac or hibiscus, which can be grown using these methods. While some people prefer evergreen species like juniper, cedar, or pine, you are not limited to the plant species you choose. In fact, you can turn a giant breed like a California redwood or sequoia into a bonsai tree! It is possible to acquire bonsai starter kits, but you can take care of your own seedlings from the launches in your own backyard. It is a personal matter to grow different types of bonsai trees. However, you can try to miniaturize all kinds that are in your local kindergarten or in your neighbor's garden. Bonsai is the art of growing trees to grow incredibly small while maintaining their size for years to come. Probably some of the most popular types of bonsai trees are the conifers. Conifers are single trees that have the appearance of antiquity from a young age. Most people who are supposed to imagine a bonsai will definitely conjure up a tree that looks like one of the pines. The shapes of the bonsai are so numerous, but the conifer is really one of the most common and practical choices. Conifers are called such simply because they normally carry cones for propagation. These types of bonsai are individuals that are typically evergreen and do not lose their leaves or even change color as the season's change. So you have a bonsai tree that is always green and has much less work for you just because it requires much less pruning and maintenance. These types of bonsai trees also grow slowly and may only require a root cut every two to three years.

Juniper trees are trees among the multitude of conifers. These trees generally have hard, peeling bark, and they also make cones for seed pods. Juniper trees are excellent as a bonsai tree because they are hardy and also great for jin bonsai trees. Jin Bonsai is an art form in which the bark of the trees is so weathered that it looks antiquated and almost looks like it could tell a story. These types of bonsai are also easy to develop and use in the sun. They are also able to bloom incredibly beautiful, white, delicate flowers. These varieties of bonsai are also available in different shades of green. They can adapt well to both the interior and the exposure outdoors. Pine trees are the types of bonsai trees that grow sturdy and extremely upright. These types of bonsai will require little attention besides pruning, but as far as sunlight and watering are concerned, they are a robust set. Some of the most common types of bonsai trees are Japanese black pine and five-needle pine. Other types of conifers that are normally used are spruce and cypress. They are just as hardy as the other conifer species and just as dignified in old age. Bonsai trees as a hobby have grown up. It is known for the amount of patience it takes to grow a beautiful bonsai. However, the hobby, as such, is fascinating, and most bonsai artists never complain about the time when miniature wonders grow there. Since a lot of time and vigor is devoted to creating a beautiful bonsai, the most experienced artists prefer to imagine the shape of their bonsai specimens before they start training the trees. Therefore, you should have clear impressions of the bonsai tree that you want to grow. If you have this idea firmly in your head, you can train the bonsai tree much better.

Consider bonsai as a gift; a bonsai is an incomparable example of a gift with lasting appeal. It is a gift with history. It is a work of art. It is the gateway to a lifelong hobby. A bonsai is a natural, environmentally friendly gift. A bonsai is alive. And perhaps the best of everything: every single bonsai is unique from the start and will become even more over the years while some bonsai are worth thousands of dollars. Now there are some rare trees that are incredibly valuable and difficult to maintain. Some trees require a lot of attention and expertise. If you reside in a cold climate, preparing an outdoor tree for winter can be challenging. But there are also many, many types of bonsai that are easy to care for. For the uninitiated, an easy-care bonsai that survives inside like any other "houseplant" in winter is probably the best place to start. The most trendy bonsai in North America is juniper. When you buy a juniper as a gift, you have to stick to Juniper procumbens unless you buy it for someone who already has a lot of bonsai. This is a special type of juniper that is ideal for bonsai, is very easy to grow, and can be brought indoors. There are some junipers - for example, the juniper chinensis that cannot be brought in. So don't be fooled.

ScheffleraArboricola - Whether you notice it or not, you saw this tree as a houseplant or in a restaurant or office. This small version of the very suitable houseplant is an interesting and easy-care bonsai. Unlike the Juniper, this bonsai doesn't look quite as Japanese, but it looks very tropical - almost like a jungle. Any friend, especially one who likes houseplants, will love this unique exotic version.

Mini Jade / Dwarf Jade - The correct name is Portulacariaafra, and it comes from South Africa. However, since so many are familiar with jade trees as houseplants, the mini jade or the dwarf jade is probably a better name. Here is another bonsai that drops its leaves when it is used too hard, but they grow back easily, and this could very well be the number one easy-to-grow bonsai. Mini Jades - like their full-size namesake - are also very attractive exotically and uniquely. It's rounded, very fleshy leaves look like something a dinosaur would have hidden behind, even though the mini jade is a very small one. Although you can never let a bonsai dry out completely, jade is one of the more forgiving little water slides. That alone would qualify you for this list, but you'll find that the mini jade bonsai, with its tiny leaves and remarkably tree-like appearance, is an excellent gift bonsai for something so small.

Fukien tea - Fukien tea (sometimes referred to as Fujian tea) is one of the classic bonsai in terms of tropical trees. It must be kept warm and must not dry out. For some reason, it is very attractive to insect pests. But with its tiny perfect, shiny, dark green leaves, white flowers, and red berries, this tree is a bonsai for bonsai lovers. For anyone who appreciates the classics, this is a gift that they will never forget.

Ficus bonsai trees, It is fun to take care of them and bring them into their individual shapes. In fact, that's one of the coolest things about bonsai: each is unique and has its own shape and personality. It is wonderful, peaceful, and relaxing to sit down with your bonsai tree to work on and exciting at the same time! If you are obsessed with bonsai, be sure to consider what type to get. Do you want one that is mainly cared for indoors? Then go with something like a ficus bonsai. They are usually cared for indoors, especially in winter. The ficus can be great from the start as it is a little easier to care for indoors and yet offers all the things that make a bonsai great! We are usually taught that bonsai trees are very rare and difficult to obtain, but this is not the case with ficus ginseng. This is quite easy to find and can even be bought in numerous chain stores or on the Internet. As you may have guessed, they are first grown in Asia and then shipped all over the world. You only have to decide on the type of pot or the size of the trunk. Ficus - There are different types of ficus, better known as figs. Other well-known fig bonsai that make good gifts are the Benjamina and the ginseng fig. The only thing everyone should know about figs is that they tend to drop leaves when they're stressed and that they can be stressed very easily. However, they will grow back! Do not give up.

HOW TO FIGURE OUT WHICH VARIETY IS BEST FOR YOUR BONSAI PROJECT - ADVICE FOR THE BEGINNER BONSAI

To qualify as a bonsai tree, it must conform to a specific shape and style. The tree must have good roots. The roots give a stable impression. When buying, make sure the tree is well anchored in the pot. Hull moves slightly from left to right. If it doesn't seem to be well-founded, choose another one. The trunk of the tree should taper. This means that the trunk must end at one point. It must have a minimum of surface scars. They must be distributed around the trunk. The largest is about 1/3 the height of the tree. Seen from the front, no branch should hide the body or the main trunk in the first 2/3 of the height. Generally, the lower branches bend down. The ones in the middle are almost horizontal and even point upwards. It should be tight and look healthy. The foliage is generally a good indicator of the health of the tree. The older a bonsai is, the higher its value. The oldest bonsai around 600 years the value is around half a million US dollars! You can choose between tropical species, hardy and semi-hardy.

The bonsai plant is available in a wide range that is available on the market. This type of plant is known today because it has aesthetic value for your home and could be a useful hobby for you. If you want to get the right plant from bonsai, you need to know the selection of these plants. These decisions will help you make the right choice so that you are proud to have the plant. And then you can use it. The placement of the facility is an important consideration to consider before you buy the facility. You can choose the tropical species of this plant that can be placed in the window. This category of plant needs a lot of light. If your home doesn't get a lot of light, you can use a fluorescent light to replace natural sunlight. You can also choose a variety of evergreen that can be placed in a window all winter. This plant cannot be placed directly in the sun. It must be placed in a shady place to avoid strong sun exposure. In addition to the two varieties above, there are many varieties of this plant that you can choose from. You should get the right information before you determine the plant that you are going to buy. You can also ask the florist about the plant for the right advice and decision, so you don't feel sorry. If you want to buy a bonsai, we recommend that you visit a garden center or tree nursery that specializes in bonsai trees. Don't make the mistake of buying your first bonsai at the grocery store because you may find a plant that has not been properly for. When choosing your bonsai, pay attention to trees or plants with shiny, lively leaves, smooth bark, and no brown spots or yellowish leaves. Several pests and fungi affect common bonsai species. It's also important to ask an expert what type of plant to buy, depending on where you keep your bonsai tree. While some bonsai artists like to present their bonsai trees indoors, most bonsai being outdoors is better. In an outdoor environment, your tree can maintain the moisture and air circulation it needs to survive, as well as the natural, seasonal temperature changes it is used to. For example, many plants have a resting phase in winter. If you want an indoor bonsai, be sure to buy a tropical species that can withstand warmer temperatures and less natural light.

There are countless ways to establish a bonsai that all ends with the same result. In reality, you have the choice to buy a bonsai tree at different stages. A tree begins as a tree seed that you can buy online. Many people retail bonsai tree seeds, but they are just ordinary tree seeds that are commonly used for bonsai. After the tree has germinated, one speaks of a tree seedling. From this point on, they are watered, fertilized, and cared for over a number of years. After the tree has fattened with minimal bonsai training for some time, they are sold as "pre-bonsai". These are trees that were kept compact for bonsai training but were not trained for a specific shape or style. These trees are for buyers who want to learn the training aspects but do not want to wait for the seed to grow. After the bonsai have been trained in shape and style, they are sold as bonsai. Most of these trees need maintenance to maintain their size. After the tree has aged well as a bonsai, they are commonly sold as "sample bonsai". These are beautiful bonsai trees that are very old and well trained. However, buying these trees is usually associated with a high price.

Always think about the art of bonsai. Bonsai are not the trees themselves but relate specifically to the process by which the trees grow and are cared for. Bonsai is an ancient art that was first thought to be practiced by Chinese who shaped their trees into animal shapes and later modified and improved by Japanese. Bonsai trees are beautiful when they grow properly and can awaken any garden with envy from friends and neighbors. You will acquire many skills when you pick up bonsai. You will acquire new plant knowledge, cutting skills as well as feeding and care skills. Bonsai definitely had its rewards. If you are in view of this or have already bought your first tree, you should carefully follow the advice. This will include some advice for the beginner bonsai. The first piece of advice for the novice bonsai is to think this through carefully before going out and buying a forest of trees. Bonsai can be very advantageous, but also very frustrating. You should first think about the time you have to spend. Nobody says that if you work full time, you cannot grow bonsai. You need to consider your work commitments and other interests and check that you can reconcile everything and still use the time for your trees. You also need to think about what to do with the trees when you go on vacation, just like a pet. The next advice for the bonsai novice is to know his own personality. Especially when it comes to patience and perseverance. Bonsai are tender and die easily. You may find your tree is doing well, but suddenly it gets worse. This kind of thing happens, and you must not let it stop you from trying again. Sometimes bonsai give the impression of decaying for no apparent reason. You may have done everything to save it and it doesn't help. That doesn't mean you're the kiss of death. It could mean that the tree had something complex, or you just have to practice. Definitely try again. You finally get it and reap the rewards.

Find out what killed your tree and take that knowledge to the next. The third piece of advice for the novice bonsai is to check that you have enough space. These trees don't grow very quickly. So if you don't live in a shoebox, you most likely have room for one. If you want to leave your trees outside, make sure there are some cool and shady spots to bring your trees to in certain periods of the intense sun or hot, dry weather. You may also want a protected area for periods of heavy rain.

Don't be fooled by the size and tenderness of these trees. There is no purpose why they cannot be kept outdoors, and most types of bonsai are better suited for outdoor use. For houseplants, make sure you have a fairly large window or balcony. Bonsai need light to survive. Be careful not to bring them near the window, as the sunlight falling through the glass will be intensified. This will bake your bonsai. The fourth piece of advice for the novice bonsai is to know the type of your tree. Contrary to trendy belief, bonsai is not a tree species, but art. There are many types of bonsai trees. Some are deciduous, and others are conifers. Knowing your tree species is crucial as the care instructions vary accordingly. Remember that they are so sensitive that there may be a mistake in the care instructions, and they are curtains for your bonsai. One final piece of advice for the bonsai novice is to start small. It is best to start with one or two trees as a whole forest. Bonsai trees are not cheap. So make yourself familiar with the care you need and keep it simple. It will be easier to deal emotionally and financially with the death of one bonsai than with twelve. Hopefully, this instruction will help you and your new business. Remember, if you don't succeed at first, try again.

HOW TO PROPERLY CARE FOR YOUR BONSAI TREE

THE BASIC RULES FOR the care of bonsai plants may not differ significantly from other basic rules for the care of other plants. On the other hand, since they are not ordinary houseplants, they need exceptional care to become healthy and beautiful. Growing bonsai trees is a wonderful and rewarding hobby, as it can encourage breeders' creativity, test their patience, and help them relax while taking care of the plant! Some studies are showing that caring for this type of miniature tree can help a person become calmer and happier. The basics of bonsai care are relatively simple and easy to follow. An enthusiast only needs to be attentive and dedicated to his hobby!

First and foremost, a grower must be fully aware of the type he or she grows. It is best to know that not all are the same and that each tree species has different needs. There are bonsai that grow well indoors, but most trees grow better outdoors. Indoor and outdoor bonsai have a variety of needs. However, the outdoors can be brought into the house for decoration; It is not advisable to keep them indoors for a long time. They can usually be kept in the house for a maximum of three days a month. If a bonsai has just been bought in a shop, it is advisable to repot it as soon as it gets home. Great care should be taken when repotting a bonsai. Many bonsai plants do not do well if they are under stressful conditions, and repotting is not excluded. Bonsai can be pruned and repotted once a year, especially in spring. However, there are some varieties of bonsai that do not need to be repotted for at least two years.

Bonsai growers should also know that taking care of the bonsai is of paramount importance when properly watering the bonsai. Bonsai has a limited root system because it is a small tree, and the care of the small tree starts from the roots. Water is critical to keeping the tree alive and healthy, but it is better to know how much water the bonsai actually needs, as there are curl species that need a lot of water, but some don't. A bonsai enthusiast should also keep in mind that when watering the bonsai, the water drains appropriately, as standing water can promote root rot and fungal growth. Another important part of bonsai care concerns the health of your tree. It is important to pay attention to growths or spots on the branches, leaves, and trunk of the bonsai, as well as discoloration, as these indicate an illness. Parasites such as insects and mites can also infect the plant, so it is better to check them regularly. Unhealthy branches and leaves, as well as the visible parasites, should be removed from the bonsai. If help is needed to restore the health of a sick bonsai, the bonsai should be taken to the nearest bonsai nursery for professional help.

Some people love flowers and plants and are now familiar with bonsai trees. Such people should know that "bonsai" is a Japanese word meaning "planted in pots" and that bonsai trees are smaller, more miniaturized versions of larger trees. The origins of the trees are in Japan and their size varies from a few centimeters to a few feet depending on the type of plant in question. First-time visitors will be surprised that these special trees, like their normal counterparts, also bear fruit and flowers. Before you learn how to care for bonsai trees, you should know more about their species. These miniature trees are available in two different versions, outdoors and indoors. Caring for bonsai trees also means that you know these different types and choose the ones that suit your environment. For example, if you plan to grow subtropical or tropical bonsai trees, make sure that you place them in a place where they can provide sufficient sunlight in the morning and shade in the evening. You should also be sure that you don't expose your trees to extreme sunlight, as many varieties of such trees cannot withstand intense heat. To properly care for bonsai trees, you should now look at the different varieties of such trees. Some of the indoor varieties include baby jade, ficus, sago palms, some elm varieties, serissa, pachira, fucia tea, and gardenia. Ask an agency that knows and takes care of bonsai trees. It will tell you that the outer varieties are divided into two different groups. The main group consists of evergreen trees such as juniper, azalea, and pine. As the name suggests, these evergreen trees keep their foliage despite the season. Generally, their rest period is during the winter season, when you can observe a yellow tinge around their leaves.

Then there are deciduous trees, and these include maple and elm. Deciduous trees tend to shed their leaves during the fall season and germinate again in spring. Although there are different types of bonsai trees, they all have one point in common, and you should recognize this if you want to take care of them. With a few rare exceptions, most bonsai trees require special care. Depending on the community climate, it may be necessary to protect them from excessive cold and heat. In addition, you have to pay attention to the humidity and try to keep it as much as possible. It is advisable to choose a bonsai plant that is suitable for the humidity in your region, rather than monitoring and changing the humidity for the tree. This is a difficult task if you are looking for an outdoor variety.

With proper care, bonsai can live for hundreds of years, with valuable specimens passed down from generation to generation, admired for their age, and venerated as a reminder of those who have cared for them over the centuries. Although these bonsai are extremely beautiful - meticulously cared for and equipped with so much knowledge over the years - age is not absolutely necessary. It is more important than the tree has the desired artistic effect, that it is in the right proportion to the appropriate container and that it is in good health. Overall, bonsai is something very personal, and there are no strict rules that need to be followed if you are just doing it as a hobby that you can enjoy. It doesn't have to be an expensive engagement, but it is an engagement that takes a lot of time, patience, skill, and persistence. Although things may not go exactly as planned, don't give up.

Potted trees can make your home or garden more aesthetic, and this is especially true for the bonsai tree variety. Of course, most people think that maintaining this diversity of trees is a complicated and tedious task. Bonsai trees come in a variety of species, but each of them follows the same basic care guidelines. It is of great importance if you want to grow these plants to understand that they all have their own requirements for water, fertilizer, light, and even the right positioning. So it is important to know what these trees need to thrive and thrive.

Caring for bonsai trees is one of the most important aspects when growing bonsai. Bonsai trees require a lot more attention and care than normal garden trees and plants. The care schedule for bonsai plants depends on the season and the type of plant. Nevertheless, it is important to know some common care tips for bonsai trees that can be used for different types of plants. The different seasons in a bonsai training calendar can be divided into spring, summer, autumn, and winter. Spring is the model time of year to start a new bonsai plant. For existing bonsai plants, it's the best time to cut and exercise. The late spring season should be used for wiring your bonsai trees.

During the summer months, place your bonsai tree in the shade of a tree in the garden. It should be placed so that it is exposed to sunlight for about 3 to 5 hours a day. Protect your bonsai from hot wind by shielding it with protective grids. Make sure your bonsai tree doesn't dry out completely, but at the same time, do not overwater your bonsai. During the midsummer period, the growth of the plant slows down, which is why you need to reduce your feeding plans. Shortly before the end of summer and autumn, it's time to prepare your trees for the upcoming winter by reducing the frequency of watering and forage. Pruning the trees should be avoided in autumn. The best feed for your bonsai plants during this time should contain a mixture of phosphorus and potassium without nitrogen. This is because nitrogen promotes plant growth and this is what we want to avoid.

Winter is the time when your bonsai would need maximum protection. Protect your bonsai plant from extreme cold and icy winds. In regions where there is insufficient sunlight during the winter season, place bonsai in a greenhouse or in the artificial growing light. The best thing you should do is to keep your plants in a cold setting during the main winter season. The word bonsai literally means "tree in a pot or tray". Some good outdoor bonsai species are Japanese maple, elm, ginkgo, juniper, and boxwood. Bonsai grown indoors require more attention and babysitting. Tropical and subtropical species such as the

Hawaiian umbrella tree, baby jade, and bush cherry are good indoor trees. All bonsai trees need good morning light, even air humidity, and adequate irrigation. Indoors, trees are often good if they are placed near a sunny window. A humidifier can help keep the air inside moist. Bonsai need to be repotted at least every two years, usually around spring, and some maintenance needs to be taken during this time. Roots must be pruned while repotting so that the bonsai remain relatively small and do not grow more than necessary. The new saucepan must have the same drainage holes as the old one, or you can repot it into the old saucepan if desired. Drainage characteristics must protect the roots from water rot, which is common in potted plants. The indoor bonsai tree itself needs to be pruned and pinched to maintain its original shape or the shape that is ideally needed. These maintenance steps are usually performed during the spring season within the locale to keep tree growth under control.

Like all other plant species, bonsai need three things to survive: sun, food, and water. Suppose your bonsai lives primarily outdoors. As a bonsai artist, your main concern is to feed and water your trees. Feeding your bonsai with the right nutrients and trace elements is crucial to promote correct and healthy growth. Improper casting is probably the most common mistake beginners make. Anyone with the right teaching resource, whether it is a master bonsai artist or a serious accountant, can easily learn how to care for their bonsai correctly. Many bonsai artists think for the first time that it's about owning a bonsai. That's not what bonsai is about. Bonsai is about the joy of looking after them and ultimately about their creation. Indeed, creating a peaceful environment in your workplace is a difficult task. It takes a lot of creative ideas and time to create such a niche. Bonsai trees are a very innovative method of interior finishing, in which miniature plants are exhibited to create a green environment. Bonsai trees are grown with the aim of creating a healthy environment, and this is the most outstanding characteristic of this tree. Growing a bonsai yourself is a lengthy process, and therefore it is recommended to decorate the interior with natural-looking artificial bonsai trees.

Training and cutting techniques will come into play. In addition, you should not use any type of soil that tends to dry out completely. Such purposes should always be considered when choosing the right soil mix for your bonsai. It is best to find out about the nature of the different floor types so that you can make the right choice. To make sure you have a healthy tree, look for glossy, vibrant leaves, as shriveled or yellowish foliage can be a symptom of pests or diseases. Make sure there are no brown spots on leaves or branches. The right container for your bonsai tree is just as important as the tree itself. Normally, evergreen plants such as cedar and pine are presented in unglazed ceramic pots in neutral or earthy colors, while deciduous trees can be placed in glazed or unglazed pots. The color of the container should set off the colors of the leaves or flowers of the bonsai. For example, a deep blue pot would highlight the bright red and orange foliage of a maple. A blooming pink bonsai can look best in a yellow or green pot. There are several traditional styles for bonsai trees: formal upright, informal upright, slant, cascade, and broom are the most common styles. Each of these styles mimics what a tree could look like in a natural setting: for example, blown away by the wind or swept down the side of a mountain. Different styles go well with each style.

Special tools are required to form a bonsai. The most basic bonsai tools include long-handled scissors, bud shears, pliers, wire cutters, root rakes, and concave cutters. To get a tree into the shape you want, you need to anchor the trunk to the roots or container with copper wire, and then gently bend the branches by wrapping them with wire and causing them to be leveled or bent. Bonsai trees need to be carefully pruned, especially in times of new growth, when shoots and buds need to be pruned to maintain tree shape. Depending on how fast the tree grows, it is also important to replant a bonsai every year. If you don't cook again, the roots can become too long, and the bonsai can become "pot-bound". When potting again, it is important to cut the roots and pot the tree in a well-drained container in well-prepared, moist soil. While many bonsai gardeners choose to buy their trees in a kindergarten for the first time, many bonsai lovers like to grow their bonsai from scratch. There are several ways to grow bonsai, but they all take a lot of time and patience. You can buy a seedling in a nursery and let it develop to the extent that you can develop it into a bonsai, or you can buy seeds, let them germinate, and then cultivate your young tree until it is malleable. Another means of propagation is to take a cut from a "parent" tree, plant it, and maintain it along. Many enthusiasts prefer to grow from cuttings because they can duplicate the genes and properties of the parent tree. Other more complex means of growing a bonsai include grafting: adding a new branch or root to an existing tree or layer, injuring the bark of a parent tree, and then helping the callus (injured part) develop a new one Bud and new roots for themselves. Growing and training a bonsai tree is really an art and can be a nice addition to your home or garden!

You can place your bonsai on a "moisture bowl" filled with decorative stones, which should always be kept moist to increase the humidity. Another solution is regular fogging. Misting or spraying is the most common method of humidification. It has the added benefit of removing dust from your bonsai, which keeps out sunlight and disrupts the exchange of oxygen and carbon dioxide. Make sure you mist with room temperature water. Keep your indoor bonsai trees away from drafty doors or windows and from heat sources such as ventilation openings, radiators or fireplaces. The bonsai environment is "artificial" and therefore requires our intervention, our help, and care to maintain the health and expansion of the bonsai tree. The easiest way to get a healthy bonsai tree, besides watering frequently, is a common dose of fertilizer for the soil. Use a balanced fertilizer to feed your bonsai tree - usually every 20-20-20 with 25% starch. The numbers 20-20-20 indicate the weight percentage of the N-P-K (nitrogen, phosphorus, and potassium) contained in this fertilizer. These elements promote the growth of your bonsai tree. N - Nitrogen is in charge of the size and quantity of the new growth and, to some extent, for the green color of the leaves. Nitrogen is needed for cell division and also for protein production. P - phosphorus is also necessary for cell division and is associated with good root growth and good flowering. K - Potassium stimulates cell enzymes and is related to the overall healthy cell activity.

All bonsai trees and shrubs need nutrients to grow. Its main nutrients are nitrogen, phosphorus, and potassium. There are other basic phytonutrients that are required for healthy, vibrant flora. These are calcium and magnesium that are normally found in the soil. If your bonsai tree soil lacks nutrients, these can be added in the form of fertilizer. The nutrients most lacking in most soils are nitrogen, phosphorus, and potassium. Therefore, most fertilizers aim to replace these three elements. The fertilizer usually also contains trace elements such as magnesium, iron, boron, copper, and zinc, which are not needed in large quantities but are essential for healthy plant growth. Fertilizers are usually available in two types; organic (derived from natural sources such as plants or animals) or inorganic (chemical-based). Both types are effective and are used extensively by bonsai tree growers. To ensure the survival and beauty of your bonsai, you must keep it free from harmful pests, diseases, and disorders. This practice requires constant inspection and vigilance as a pest problem can occur at any time. Correct handling of pests and diseases is an important part of bonsai horticulture. The key to success in tackling these common problems is your ability to identify the symptoms of the pest, disease, or disorder and use the right remedy. Understand how each of these key ingredients works and how to provide what is needed when it is needed. Success in growing bonsai does not depend on one element but on the right combination of all. This is important. Different types of bonsai have different needs and preferences. There are two problems with irrigation, either it's above or underwater the bonsai tree. The effects of under irrigation are fairly easy to see while the effects of overwatering can last significantly longer.

The right soil for bonsai trees

Choosing the right floor is crucial for indoor bonsai care

- after all, half of the tree is covered with soil. To choose the right soil type, you should go to your nearest garden center (or a bonsai specialist near you) and tell them the exact type of your bonsai tree. They help you find the right floor for your needs. Also, remember to buy the highest quality floor as this makes a big difference. To be honest, there is no solid shape or a combination of soil that is suitable for all types of bonsai. The successful growth of a bonsai depends to a large extent on other factors that affect the tree type, the weather conditions, and the location. Therefore, for best results, it is advisable to speak to a reputable bonsai dealer. In the meantime, here are some common facts about the main components of a good quality bonsai floor. This information can help you choose the right soil for your trees:

Organic materials can store moisture and fertilize plants. In addition, they can enable environmental activities that are essential for maintaining the health of plants. Examples of organic elements are pine bark, peat moss, leaf mold, and coffee grounds. A disadvantage of using pure organic components is that they tend to retain too much moisture, which causes the plants to suffocate. For this, it is better to mix in some inorganic elements to allow free air circulation. Such elements consist of semi-porous and non-porous components that play different important roles for the proper growth of bonsai trees. The semi-porous components not only enable free air circulation but also generate water vapor. This is particularly helpful for trees that cannot absorb water in liquid form. Examples of inorganic elements are lava rock, hid rocks, and haydite. As mentioned earlier, one of the leading purposes of the soil is to keep the plants upright. The use of non-porous components serves this purpose. Examples of these components are sharp gravel and river sand. Overall, it's safer to say that good bonsai soil should be a mix of organic and inorganic compounds. Such a combination is important in order to achieve better plant growth. Each component has a specific role that is critical to maintaining the health of bonsai trees.

While you can make your own blend of bonsai soil, different types of soil for certain tree species are available on the market. Akadama: this is the most common type of soil and is suitable for deciduous trees. Kureyu: this type of soil is perfect for conifers. Kanuma: suitable for azaleas and acid-loving bonsai trees. When caring for plants, especially bonsai trees, choosing the right type of soil is very important. Bonsai plants are fragile, and it takes patience, discipline, and determination to care for them. Maintaining a bonsai garden is neither a hobby nor a short course that may just be coming to an end. Growing bonsai trees is a job of love. It is an art that takes a long time to be perfect. Keep in mind that you must have all of the aforementioned intellectual and emotional qualities in order to maintain a bonsai garden successfully. Some trees need to be protected from the weather in winter. The techniques used depend on how well the tree is adapted to the climate. During the winter, temperate species are allowed to go into hibernation. However, care should be taken with deciduous plants that they do not break their idle state too soon. In-ground cold rooms, unheated garages, porches and the like are usually used, or by mulching the plant in its container to the depth of the first branch or by burying it with the root system under the frost line.

Using a useful bonsai soil is a crucial component in trying to keep your bonsai tree strong. Finding a very good bonsai soil is a time-consuming process for the novice. For the experienced bonsai arborist, great soil helps to distinguish a flowering, healthy tree from a tree that only stays alive for a few months to a year. When choosing bonsai soil, there are a few things to consider, regardless of whether you are an experienced gardener or not. Bonsai need fast-draining soil that maintains its shape to stay alive. As a result of the small footprint of a bonsai tree, root rot is much more likely to occur if you don't have excellent soil. Root rot is a death sentence for a bonsai tree and can quickly ruin the growth of your tree for years. In addition, poorly selected floors tend to break apart and clean the roots annually. This is particularly harmful to pine bonsai trees and juniper. If you want to use floors that are prone to break apart or rot, like organic soil for example, you need to make sure that the tree you use for this type of soil can handle root bearings at least once or twice a year.

Probably the most popular type of bonsai soil on the market is inorganic soil. It is fired clays that keep their shape and absorb moisture well from which the roots can then feed. This is important because these soils have good drainage that prevents root rot from occurring. Since the highest quality baked clay is usually absorbent there is enough moisture for the roots to get what they need while the excess drains away. This type of inorganic soil is suitable for many types of bonsai. If you don't know where to look, getting great bonsai soil can be a challenge. Bonsai soil can be spotted in the most unusual places, including hardware stores, auto parts stores, and pet stores. Online bonsai tree traders usually purchase their floors from these locations and make blends that are ideal for certain tree species. Whenever you get bonsai soil, it is important that you simply test the soil before using it. High-quality floors don't break down so easily. You shouldn't be able to easily crush it in your hand or break it when it's poured into water and then frozen. Bonsai soils that are broken down in this way usually do not last long and can cause problems with certain tree species.

Although bonsai trees need constant care, feeding, care, and maintenance to keep them in good condition, no horticultural qualification is required to grow bonsai successfully. If you tilt it correctly, your bonsai can live well. According to Japanese bonsai tree growers, learning the right bonsai irrigation technique takes a lifetime. The role air plays in the physiology of plants is rarely recognized or valued. The synthesis process absorbs carbon dioxide from the air through the leaves of the plant and combines it with water to make starch and sugar for the plant's nutrition. This is possible because the plant uses the energy of the sun's rays. The bonsai roots also need air, but the root system uses them differently. Water and nutrients are absorbed into the plant by the fine root hairs that grow on the tips of the bonsai roots. The root hairs can only absorb water in the form of water vapor, and this steam can only be generated if there is air. This is why the irrigation process of the bonsai is so important. If the soil is flooded or compacted so that the air is partially or completely excluded, the roots cannot absorb moisture, and the tree dies. Good bonsai soil is a soil through which air can flow freely.

There are two different ways to clean up - "root clean up" and "branch clean up". Root cutting should take place at the beginning of spring, and only when the roots of the bonsai are grounded in the pot. Simply select the germs you want to keep and remove the bad ones. The branches should also be cut shortly before the beginning of spring. Select the branches you want to keep and carefully remove the others. Proper pruning is one of the most important factors when caring for bonsai trees indoors. Without proper control, for example, you cannot bring your bonsai tree into different shapes. Tree care is picking and spreading the right fertilizer and soil. To find the right floor, go to your local garden center and tell the staff exactly what type of bonsai you have. They will then guide you to the right type of soil. Please note that it is definitely worth buying soil that is as expensive as possible since high-quality soil absorbs nutrients from fertilizers better and thus creates a better living environment for your bonsai tree. To pick fertilizer properly, make sure you buy high quality, water-soluble fertilizer that contains a good variety of nutrients. Fertilizers should only be used through the growing season and should only be used when the soil is damp, or they lose their effectiveness.

Opinions about soil mixtures and fertilization vary widely among practitioners. Some advocate the use of organic fertilizers to promote an essentially inorganic soil mix, while others use chemical fertilizers freely. Bonsai soils are designed to optimize drainage. Bonsai soil is primarily a loose, fast-flowing mixture of components, often a basic mixture of coarse sand or gravel fired clay pellets or expanded slate, combined with an organic component such as peat or bark. In Japan, clay-based volcanic soils (Akadama or "red ball" soils and Kanuma, a kind of yellow pumice stone) are preferred. The soil your bonsai needs is different from your normal garden soil. Normal garden soil tends to absorb too much moisture and is too compact for bonsai. The soil suitable for bonsai is so loose that the air can reach the roots and can contain some moisture to nourish the tree. It should go well to avoid root rot and have a neutral pH. Bonsai soil consists of organic and inorganic substances. Soil mixtures for bonsai usually contain 75% inorganic, 25% organic substances, and can vary depending on the needs of your bonsai. You can use clay, gravel, or sand as an inorganic component, and mulch, and dead plant matter as an organic component.

The soil you choose for your potted bonsai tree provides it with nutrients, stores water, and plays a main role in its overall health. You need to find the right soil mix if you want your tree to thrive. Bonsai arborists have both organic and inorganic soil mixtures available. Organic soil mixtures consist of dead leaves, peat, bark, and other parts of plants. Inorganic mixtures are made from substances such as lava and clay. Soil mixtures with a high inorganic content can prove to be better for the health of the bonsai because they drain the plant better and provide it with more oxygen. Soils with high organic content tend to retain too much water, and their particles degrade over time, so less air gets into the plant. Good bonsai soils should contain a mixture of particles of different sizes, such as sand, sand, and peat, and contain enough water to keep the plant hydrated between watering, ensuring adequate drainage. Special inorganic soils for bonsai are Akadama, and porous Japanese fired clay that is mixed with sand and is the perfect medium for growing pine and other bonsai. You can find this in a bonsai kindergarten. Seramis is another type of baked clay that is easier to find and cheaper than Akadama and can be mixed with peat or bark. It promotes root growth and is stronger than Japanese clay. Different types require different water, nutrients, and soils. Coniferous bonsai-like juniper and pine need less moisture, so they need a soil that contains less water. Conversely, tropical flowering plants often need more water and, therefore, a soil that stores water better. Ask an expert in a bonsai nursery for a floor recommendation for your special bonsai species.

HOW TO PROPERLY WATER YOUR BONSAI

If you under-water your bonsai, the tree will naturally dehydrate and eventually die. If you over-water it, the tree will "drown." To properly water your bonsai, you should wait until the bottom of the pot/container begins to dry out at the top. Next, water until excess liquid comes out of the bottom of the pot/container. Do not water the bonsai again until the soil begins to dry out. If you follow this step, you will find that the tree is neither dehydrated or overhydrated. These are two of the main reasons for the pruning of bonsai trees properly. The "best" way to water is to wet the soil a little first. This improves the soil's ability to absorb a large amount of water. Then you should water efficiently until the soil is saturated. Make sure that all of the ground gets wet each time you water and wait for the excess to drain from the drainage holes to be sure. The "best" time to water is probably early in the morning before the bonsai begins its day of growing activity. Also, check during the day whether the bonsai tree is in a particularly hot and dry place. Bonsai trees do not develop when the soil is too wet and they do not grow when the soil is too dry. In the meantime, a bonsai tree absorbs water and nutrients. Develop a reasonable and realistic watering plan and try to create a regular maintenance plan for your bonsai tree. Pour your bonsai with room temperature tap water. If the water is too hot or too cold, it can shock the roots of the tree. If you have the ability, the opportunity and the time to collect rainwater is great. Moisture helps reduce water loss through perspiration. Perspiration negatively affects your bonsai's ability to retain water and stay healthy. The sometimes dry climate of a house or apartment can be changed to promote your bonsai tree.

Always water your bonsai meticulously before fertilizing and never use fertilizer on a dry tree. Over-watering is also usually much more difficult to diagnose. The immediate way to kill a bonsai tree is to let the compost dry out completely underwater. Established plants that grow in the soil have the innate ability to adapt to their environment and amount of water. When the tree needs additional water, its roots expand in search of water. Plants that grow in drier areas tend to have much larger root constructions. However, when a plant is compulsory to grow in a pot like a bonsai tree, the tree lacks the potential for the root structures to spread beyond the pot's borders in search of extra water. In other words, bonsai trees that grow in a pot need to regulate the water of the plant. Once a bonsai tree or any tree or plant shows the effects of under-watering, it is often behind time to save the tree by adding extra water. In fact, putting in the water at this point can actually do more damage to the tree. Water can be extracted from the tree through a process known as reverse osmosis. A bonsai tree that suffers from irrigation shows damage to the leaves, branch roots, and trunk. Leaves dry out and fall off the branches, the branches themselves become brittle and break easily. When the bonsai tree has been overwatered, the roots and the compost that surrounds the roots are permanently damp. A healthy tree must be able to draw oxygen into its roots. This oxygen usually comes from the compost around the roots. However, if the compost is permanently damp, it cannot absorb air. This causes the roots to die, followed by the tree's death.

So the question is: how, as a bonsai enthusiast, do you learn to water your bonsai properly? The easiest way may sound strange, but the easiest is, "never water your bonsai on a routine". Alternatively, learn to water your bonsai only when the tree needs it. On an extremely hot, dry day, your bonsai may need additional water. In other cases, the tree may not need additional water for a few days. Check the compost to determine when your tree actually needs water. The compost changes color and looks as soon as it starts to dry out. When the color of the compost turns and the top of the compost has dried out, it's time to water your bonsai tree. Morning is the best time of day to water your bonsai. This allows the water to be absorbed into the compost. The root structure before sun exposure and the heat at noon affect the tree. Watering in the last minutes of the afternoon or in the evening is not recommended unless the bonsai has dried up during the day. The soil in which you plant bonsai can affect how much and how often you need to water. For most bonsai trees that come from commercial nurseries, the pot is filled with compost. The compost keeps the water longer than an inorganic soil. It is, therefore, imperative to monitor the compost regularly to avoid over-watering. If possible, it is recommended to replace the compost with an inorganic soil, as this soil reduces the possibility of watering over. However, the majority of growers do not recommend repotting a bonsai for the first year. Some sources suggest that you water the bonsai by "dipping" it.

DO NOT water by immersion. Immersion irrigation is used to bring water into a plant with very poor quality compacted organic soil. If the bonsai actually requires to be watered by immersion, it is really in trouble. If you want to resolve this issue, drill small holes in the soil so that the water can penetrate the soil and repot the plant as soon as possible. Watering should only be done if the plant actually needs to be watered. The plant is not above or underwater. When you are watering the bonsai tree, be sure to water from the top of the tree. Then relax and enjoy your bonsai tree. Because of the type of soil on which bonsai trees grow, frequent watering is an indispensable part of bonsai care. Instructions on how often to water vary depending on the sample. In many cases, careful observation of your plant is required to determine the correct schedule. A sure hint that your bonsai needs water is to touch the ground. When the soil is dry, water it.

HOW TO SHAPE AND STYLE YOUR BONSAI PLANTS FOR ULTIMATE HEALTH AND LONGEVITY

Pruning is another important part of indoor bonsai care. The cut is made in two different ways ("branch cut" and "root cut"). At the beginning of spring, you should carefully remove all branches of the tree, except those that you want to keep. Pruning the roots is similar, but should only be done if the roots of the bonsai have settled in the pot. It is absolutely important to learn the basic process of bonsai tree pruning before trying to shape your tree in different shapes. So make sure you do these basic things, right! There are few plants that are more fascinating and beautiful than a tree in bonsai. Like every living thing, it has a growth cycle. The point of bonsai is to make sure that the growth is such that it simulates the appearance of a fully grown tree in miniature. How do you do this without taking the life of the plant? For a beautiful plant, you want to make sure your bonsai stays healthy. Since it is a tree, if you take good care of it, it can live for a long time. To ensure the longevity of your bonsai, you need to trim your bonsais properly. Don't be afraid to crop your bonsai plant. Many beginners are afraid of killing their bonsai tree by pruning. That is not a problem. To preserve a bonsai healthy and beautiful, you need to cut the tree. The first important step is to know where and when to cut the bonsai plant. This depends on what type of bonsai tree you have. The common rule is to make sure you don't prune a bonsai plant when the sap comes up. A bonsai is a tree in which sap rises like any other tree in a forest or orchard. So never cut your bonsai plant in spring! If your bonsai tree is a deciduous tree (which means that it loses its leaves in autumn), late autumn is the ideal time to prune your bonsai plant. If you have an evergreen plant, cut your bonsai plant in late winter.

Before you trim your bonsai, take a close look at it. Are there branches that look sick? Are you looking for precise shape and effect? Bonsai is a mixture of art and science. While you want to shape your bonsai for health and longevity, and you want it to be beautiful too! The first branches you choose when pruning your bonsai tree are certainly any sick or dead branches that appear to be endangering the health of the plant. While a definite amount of "driftwood" effect is fine for an aesthetic effect, make sure that it doesn't affect the health of the bonsai plant. If you have carefully observed your bonsai plant, you will have noticed which branches have produced good leaves or needles and which ones seem to be fighting. For bonsai longevity, it is best to cut off struggling branches and let the sap of the next season rise into the healthy branches for maximum health. Once you've decided on a branch, take your sharp scissors and cut the branches clean. After cutting away everything you want, seal the slits on the bonsai plant with a good tree sealant. If you have an evergreen, it is preferable to use graft wax. You can get both in every good garden center. Next fall or winter, make sure you sharpen your pruning shears and have everything ready to cut your bonsai for ultimate growth and longevity!

Trimming is indispensable for the care of bonsai trees. Bonsai has different forms, and such forms must be maintained by proper trimming. It is best to contact a bonsai expert to learn basic trimming methods. Again, this isn't limited to indoor bonsai trees. All bonsai plants must be cut correctly. Bonsai itself is a little difficult to maintain. When trimming bonsai, make sure that you get an even impression. If you cut off too many branches while ignoring the trunk, the tree will grow awkwardly. It will do this to balance itself out. The following season, it may look strange and not at all as you planned. To prevent this, shorten the trunk proportionally to the branches and vice versa. In other words, be sure to balance the height of the tree with the width so that it looks natural. The bonsai trimming tools you use for your tree should be appropriate for the size of the tree. You don't want to use large scissors to cut a miniature tree. You also need thicker blades to cut off the branches of a full-sized bonsai effectively. The blades should be short and sharp so that they can make clean cuts. Blunt blades can damage the tree, especially when used on the trunk. After trimming your bonsai, you can use the training wire to force the branches of your bonsai tree to develop in a certain way. Bonsai specialists sometimes use this material when they want a specific look for their tree. It won't harm the branches of the tree at all. Attach the wire to a section of the branch, then attach it to another branch or tree trunk, depending on which direction you want it to grow. Be careful when trying to wire your branches. If the tree is dehydrated, slightly bending the branch can cause the branch to break off. Also, make sure your bonsai is in a strong and healthy condition before using the Wire Training Technique.

One of the main features of a bonsai tree is its shape. A bonsai tree can take on a special artform due to its unique style and shape. Each person has their own choice of how they want to shape their growing bonsai tree. A bonsai tree can be shaped in many interesting ways, including popular forms such as literati, formal and informal maintenance, inclination, forest, and cascading. There are other tree styles that you can try once you learn the basics. Literati style is known as the most common form of a bonsai tree. It has a bare trunk with very small branches. The branches of this style are close to the top of the tree, and the bottom of the tree has a twisted shape. The formal and informal upright style offers a different shape. These styles are another common approach to bonsai shaping. You have a tapered trunk in a straight upright position. The informal style of this tree has bends and curves in the tree, as opposed to the formal shape that makes it look different. The oblique shape of the bonsai tree corresponds to the formal upright shape due to its straight trunk. The difference with the sloping bonsai tree is that the trunk has a slope that runs in one direction or another near the base of the tree. The forest style of the bonsai tree is created by placing multiple bonsai trees in an area or container. This is an advanced type of bonsai gardening. You can have bonsai trees of different heights with this style to give the grouping a special effect. Most people use three trees in a container to get the shape of a forest.

One of the most appealing forms of the bonsai tree is the cascade shape. This shape resembles the trees in the mountains or over water. They look very attractively shaped in cascade style. These are some of the most common styles and shapes of the bonsai tree. There are other styles you should try if you prefer something that doesn't conform to the norm. If this is your earliest, it's a good idea to start with a common style to better understand how to do it. If you successfully master common styles of this bonsai, you can try other styles.

HOW TO PROPERLY REPOT YOUR BONSAI TREE

Now that you have one of those beautiful miniature trees you've always dreamed of, you need to learn how to take good care of it. The first thing you need to do is to check the roots of the tree. Slowly take it out of the pot and see if they are in good condition. If they are dry or too big for the pot, you can simply repot them into a larger container. Remember to put high-quality bonsai soil in the new pot. If you repot a ficus ginseng bonsai, make sure you can put it in a sunny and warm place, but if you can't, wait for spring or summer to repot it. When it comes to casting, it can get more difficult. You need to water your bonsai depending on the moisture content of your soil. Your tree should never be soaked or dry. Either way, your bonsai becomes uncomfortable and becomes clear through the health of its leaves. You can water it every other day, but if you find out that the soil dries too quickly, you can water it every day. As with any other plant, sunlight is required. However, it should not be unprotected to strong sunlight for too long. It is best to leave your bonsai outside in the morning. Alternatively, you can also use an artificial lighting system. First of all, you should choose good soil for your bonsai. You should also pay attention to the correct maintenance of the floor. Apply good fertilizer quality and mild fungicide. Make sure that the fungicide is diluted in water before applying it to the soil.

Such practice is important, but not limited to it. This is

not optional. Therefore, maintaining indoor bonsai is a bigger challenge, but on the other hand, you will absolutely make it if you have enough engagement in what you do. This commitment is then rewarded with the various advantages that you can draw from this wonderful part of nature. The blooming background of bonsai, some of us have just started to notice bonsai trees. These miniaturized tiny trees, strangely shaped, suddenly seem to appear everywhere. Even if they are enjoying sudden popularity, the bonsai tree is hardly a new invention.

Your bonsai tree needs to be repotted occasionally. The root of the plant can begin to be bound and affected. If the plant roots become too thick, there is no longer enough soil around the root system to keep it moist. The bonsai do not grow under these conditions. How often the plant has to be repotted depends entirely on its growth rate. Some bonsai grow faster than others. Remove the plant from the ground to repot the bonsai tree. Remove all smaller root systems. Repot the plant into a larger holder with a suitable mixture of potting soil. This is an important part of bonsai tree care and should, therefore, be carried out regularly. This task helps refresh the soil and also eliminates the risk of your tree starving. Several factors primarily determine the regularity of repotting your bonsai tree, and all depend on the condition of the tree. Young and fast-growing bonsai trees may require this process once in a few years. Much larger trees that have matured must be repotted every 5 years. In order to find out when is the best time for your tree, you should examine it in the spring. If the roots protrude from the ground, this is an indication that the tree is looking for fresh nutrients. This means that your bonsai tree needs a pot.

Bonsai trees are living organisms and, like other living things, can be susceptible to diseases and pests. Some of these attacks occasionally affect the beauty of the tree, while sometimes they can damage the tree or even kill it if not checked. The main aspects that trigger these occurrences are relining, overfeeding, or over-watering. If your plant has yellow leaves that will eventually fall off, this may indicate an irrigation or feeding problem. If this change suddenly occurs, you can conclude that you are not giving it enough water. When this change begins to happen, it usually means that you may be over or underfeeding your bonsai plant. Pests like to feed on these plants, and you may notice grasshoppers, bees, ants, or snails visually. Aphids, wasps, mites, and weevils work more covertly and can be difficult to spot. Fungi and some types of viruses can also seriously infect these plants. These usually manifest themselves in the rapid death of the leaves and branches of the bonsai tree. In such cases, you need to quarantine the affected plant quickly and try to cure it with fungicides.

You need to start with a training pot. You will later repot the bonsai in its permanent container, so you don't have to spend too much on the practice container, and it doesn't have to look so pretty. Cascading bonsai plants should be trained in deeper pots. Tall bonsai land in flat spots, so start them in fairly flat containers. Whichever bonsai training container you choose, make sure the drain holes are at least half an inch in diameter. You can find a selection of bonsai pots in any decent garden center or kindergarten. If you look online, there is an incredible selection. Traditional bonsai pots are round, oval, square, hexagonal, or rectangular. As you can imagine, there are all sorts of crazy shapes and sizes these days. Bonsai cascade and semi-cascade types look good in round or rectangular pots. Place the plant slightly off-center (about a third from the edge). If the pot is too large, the aesthetic balance is disturbed. As a rule of thumb, the bottom of the pot should correspond approximately to the thickness of the hull. However, you also use your eye to judge. In terms of length, you want to choose a container whose length is approximately two thirds the height of the tree. If the tree is wider than it is tall, choose a planter about two-thirds the width of the tree. Remember that no pot is permanent, so you can set up a new pot as the tree grows. You can determine if a bonsai needs to be re-registered if the water takes a long time to flow through the ground or if the roots start to collect.

Repotting is a delicate exercise. You don't want to kill your bonsai tree by pulling too hard on the trunk. Carefully lift the tree out and carefully unravel the roots with a chopstick or knitting needle. Start at the edge and performance your way around slowly. Try to "comb" the roots instead of pulling them because you don't want to damage the main root. Once the bonsai plant is cleared, spray the roots with water to make sure they don't dry out and to remove the old soil. You may need to cut off the thick, old, brown roots that limit the growth of the young 'feeder' roots. Obviously, don't cut off too many. If you cut more than half of the roots, you'll probably have it over. Get your new pot now and cover the drainage holes with a simple wire mesh. This prevents the tree from falling over in the wind. Run some wire through the drainage holes and leave it for later wiring. You will probably use pliers for this.

First, apply a thin layer of gravel to aid drainage before adding the soil. Then create a small mound of earth. You can now carefully nest your bonsai on the mound of earth before evenly spreading the roots on the ground. Make sure you're happy with the position and angle of the bonsai, take the wires you've threaded and twist them on top of the main root ball. Refill with the chopstick or knitting needle to integrate the roots. You can now water the bonsai and add a little more soil if necessary, so you can promptly and easily select the right container for your bonsai and ensure that it is potted correctly. With tender love, patience, and the right methods, you will enjoy your bonsai for many years. Bonsai need to be repotted. Choosing slow-growing is the best to start with. A Juniper Bonsai is the best choice for slow-growing and a great bonsai for beginners! The bigger the bonsai, the bigger the pot has to be. You see, it's not that difficult, is it? Bonsai trees can be so rewarding if you use a step-by-step guide to growing bonsai. A step-by-step guide is the best way to learn how to care for your bonsai. Just be ready to spend time with them, and you will be rewarded.

HOW TO FERTILIZE A BONSAI TREE FOR MAXIMUM HEALTH AND GROWTH

Fertilize with a balanced tree fertilizer. Remember, bonsai are not houseplants. Fertilizer must be carefully monitored. Fertilization is usually very light and usually occurs in the spring, just before new growth begins. During the summer, the bonsai may need to be watered daily, depending on the exposure and the container size used. Never fertilize an ill tree as fertilizer is not a medication. If you are not sure of the dosage of fertilizer to use, follow the advice on the label, and never use more than approved. Fertilizer is good, but too much is a bad thing. Bonsai plants require more special care than the average houseplant. However, this does not mean that you need to be intimidated by maintaining a healthy bonsai tree. Some people think the bonsai plant is deliberately starved to keep it small, but bonsai doesn't work that way! The short size of the bonsai tree is due to the correct trimming of the roots and the training of the plant. Bonsai are little, but to have a beautiful bonsai, it must be a healthy plant. How much and what kind of fertilizer a bonsai plant needs depends on what type of plant you have, how old it is, and what time of year you fertilize your bonsai plant. A good fertilizer has the right balance of nitrogen, phosphorus, potassium, calcium, sulfur, and magnesium. Just because it's important to fertilize a bonsai plant for maximum health, it's also important to know that over-fertilizing a bonsai tree can "burn" the leaves and roots. If a bonsai tree is fertilized too often, the burned roots will not be able to draw water from the soil into the trunk, branches, and leaves. So be careful. It is always better to feed the bonsai several times with a weak solution than to overfeed it once with a solution that is too strong. The younger a plant is, the more important and more often it has to be fed like children. As the bonsai tree ages, it becomes established and uses fertilizer less and less. For a younger bonsai plant, it should be fed a few times a month, then once a month, and then once in the season the bonsai tree ages. It is also important to adapt the type of fertilizer to the needs of the bonsai plant during the growing season. In spring, when the bonsai tree reaches its peak, use a fertilizer with higher nitrogen content. Release the nitrogen in summer and feed your bonsai plant with a fertilizer that contains less nitrogen during the rest period of the year. Like humans, the more active a bonsai tree is, the more energy it needs, but overfeeding is not good for it. Always water your bonsai plant first before applying the fertilizer. This prevents root burns and prepares the bonsai tree so that it can pull the nutrients out of the ground.

There are two basic types of fertilizers: inorganic and organic. Inorganic fertilizers are the varieties that you can find in your nursery store that are either supplied in the sticks or must be mixed with water. Do not use the stick-in-the-soil type of a bonsai plant. The soil and root system of a good bonsai plant is far too flat to dissolve the stick fertilizer without burning leaves and roots. Instead, get the variety that is mixed with the water you give your plant when watering. Manure and compost are two specimens of organic fertilizers. While it is often considered the best when plants are fed organically, the use of organic fertilizer in bonsai trees should be limited to repotting. It is important not to disturb the soil of a bonsai tree too often, and for organic fertilizers to be effective, it is important that they are incorporated into the soil. To enjoy your bonsai tree, you need to fertilize your bonsai plant for maximum health. Make sure you feed it carefully so that you can always enjoy the beauty of your bonsai plants. Another thing to do when taking care of your bonsai is to apply the right type of fertilizer at the right time. Fertilizers can help your tree get enough nutrients from the soil, especially during periods of strong growth. There are many different types of fertilizers, and it can be a little difficult to find one that is suitable for your bonsai. This is because experts are often divided on the subject. Fertilizer is often used in phases of vigorous growth, as is the case with most trees in spring and summer. When applying fertilizer, take your cue from your bonsai tree. Monitor how much fertilizer you are giving and adjust your feeding accordingly.

Trees growing in the wild use their roots to get the essential nutrients they need. This constantly causes these roots to expand when all of the nutrients in that particular soil have been depleted. Bonsai trees do not have this talent because they are grown in pots. This means that you need to restore all of the nutrients by applying fertilizer. This crucial part of bonsai tree care can have a huge impact on the growth of your plant. Fertilizer products are grouped according to their nitrogen/phosphorus/potassium composition. At the beginning of spring, a mixture with more nitrogen is ideal for promoting growth. A balanced mix can be particularly good in summer. A reduced nitrogen composition supports the preparation of the plant for winter. Potassium, in turn, promotes the blooming of the flowers of a bonsai tree. Although one can think that increasing the fertilizer intensity for the bonsai results in a higher and faster growth rate, in reality, this can have negative effects and put a heavy burden on the bonsai. There comes a point where too much is exactly that, too much, and the fertilizer begins to take advantage of the original effect it was intended for and begins to do more harm than good. Overdosing the fertilizer with your bonsai can lead to a toxic effect, make it more susceptible to disease, abnormal unbalanced growth, and nutrient imbalances. Knowing and studying the specific types of bonsai that you work with is the first step to optimize your fertilizer routine and prevent you from excessive damage to your bonsai. The plant growth is different, and depending on the season, the plant has the greatest growth and requires additional nutrients. Fertilizer feeding in times of doormats or times of slow growth is not only senseless but can also be catastrophic. Depending on the maturity of your bonsai, the amount of fertilizer it needs is also determined. Young bonsai need more fertilizer than their slower-growing mature counterparts. You cannot make a doormat tree grow by adding fertilizer. The absorption rates of nutrients by plant roots also vary depending on several factors: salinity in the soil and high levels of other nutrients. Fertilizers specially made for all types of bonsai are the best choice for any bonsai artist.

Fertilizing your tree is essential for it to grow properly. After seeing the first sign of leaves, you can apply fertilizer. First, use a mild starch fertilizer. Use a balanced diet within a few months of the growing season then use a nitrogen-free bonsai fertilizer at the end of the summer season. This is used to prepare for the winter season. Make a schedule and stick to it. Know the needs of your bonsai tree and know how to grow it. When the growing season comes, it is even more important to know. During the winter season, the bonsai is fed once a month. However, you need to check if it grows before you do that. There are three numbers you need to know. You can find them on the fertilizer — the first stands for nitrogen. The higher the number, the more the foliage grows and has more green color in the leaves. The second number stands for phosphorus. Potassium is the third number. You can also use an organic brand of bonsai fertilizer. This will help because it contains everything your bonsai needs. Organic fertilizers use natural ingredients that are beneficial to the health of your bonsai. Other fertilizers with chemicals can be toxic and cause the nutrients to be produced slowly. You can also use slow-release pellets for your bonsai. People use them when they forget to fertilize their bonsai. The pellets are placed on the floor. The nutrients are penetrated in small portions. For this reason, they are effective in the soil for at least 30 days. If you can stick to a schedule well, you should use liquid fertilizer. When the soil is watered, the nutrients are washed away. Because of this short timeframe, the liquid is applied for at least three to six weeks during the season when you don't grow bonsai. The liquid fertilizer should be applied to the leaves and penetrate the soil. During the growth phase, place slow-release pellets on the floor for feeding and feed the liquid fertilizer every two weeks during this time. If you find that your bonsai tree does not meet the requirements, do not apply fertilizer. When the soil is dry, do not put any fertilizer on it. It is important that watering and fertilizing go hand in hand.

LISTEN TO THE AUDIOBOOK FOR FREE

DID YOU KNOW YOU CAN DOWNLOAD THE AUDIOBOOK VERSION OF THIS BOOK FOR FREE?

- VISIT **BIT.LY/BONSAI-US** FOR AUDIBLE US
- VISIT **BIT.LY/BONSAI-UK** FOR AUDIBLE UK

BONSAI CONTAINER

First, look for a pot with an attractive shape that fits your tree. Does your tree cascade? Is it asymmetrical? Is it leaning in a certain direction? Consider all of these nuances when choosing a tree. Similarly, choose a pot color that matches the color of the leaves of the tree. If it is a flowering bonsai, choose a pot color that matches the flower color. Second, look at the function of the pot. A bonsai pot should be flat. This keeps the roots flat, and the tree small - just like a bonsai should be. Remember seven years in the pot equals one year in the soil. The pot should have large drainage holes and wiring holes. The roots remain ventilated through the drainage holes, and the cable openings allow you to place the bonsai exactly where you want them in the pot. There are no wiring holes in the cheap pots for artificial trees. They glue artificial bonsai in the pot. Each bonsai pot is equipped with drainage holes so that the excess water can drain off. Each hole is usually covered with a plastic strainer or grille to prevent dirt from escaping. Containers come in different shapes and colors (glazed or unglazed). Most evergreen bonsai are located in unglazed pots, while deciduous trees are planted in glazed pots. It is necessary that the color of the pot matches the tree. Bonsai pots are made all over the world, some are of higher quality than others, and some are highly collectible, like old Chinese or Japanese pots, which are made in highly advertised regions with experienced pot makers like Tokoname, Japan. Highly collectible pots are not limited to Asia, however. European artists like Byran Albright and Gordon Duffett make unique pots that bonsai artists collect. Pre-bonsai materials are often placed in "growth boxes" made from scraps of fence boards or wooden slats. These large boxes permit the roots to grow more freely and increase the strength of the tree. The second phase, after using a grow box, is to plant the tree in a "practice box". This is often smaller and helps to build a smaller, dense root mass that can be easily moved into a final presentation pot.

A ceramic bonsai pot should be just big enough to fully support your bonsai tree and provide space for a little growth. Choose a pot that complements your tree and does not steal focus. The art of bonsai is to replicate a naturally growing tree as closely as possible but on a much smaller scale. So make sure that your bonsai pot is proportionate to your tree, has an asymmetrical design, and has a neutral color. Another important aspect is to make sure that the bonsai pot has enough holes for drainage. All too often, bonsai trees get wet or dry out due to different water levels or insufficient water drainage. You will also be well advised to choose a ceramic bonsai pot that is not glazed inside. A bonsai pot that is shiny on the inside can cause major problems with heat storage in the ground and, in turn, affect the watering. However, it is okay to choose a bonsai pot that is glazed from the outside. Just make sure the pot is frost-proof if your bonsai tree lives outside. Shiny Surface Bonsai pots that are not designed for bad weather are notorious for cracks.

The pot in which you place your bonsai should

complement the shape and style of the tree. The size, color, and design of the container should all be considered. While you can train your bonsai in an informal tray or box, a fully shaped tree should be displayed in a formal bonsai container. This is usually ceramic stoneware that can be glazed or unglazed in different colors and sizes. All bonsai pots should have drainage holes in the bottom to drain excess water. Your bonsai pot should be resistant to both heat and cold. Most stoneware pots are fired to withstand temperature fluctuations. If you know your bonsai is outdoors in an extreme climate, it's best to choose an unglazed pot. If your bonsai is only indoors, you can use a porcelain pot that gives an elegant look to a flowering tree. Color is an important consideration. Most bonsai gardeners choose unglazed, rustic, earth-tone pots for outdoor bonsai such as evergreens and pines, while a colorful, glazed pot can highlight flowering or fruit-bearing trees such as brush cherries. The shape and depth of the container should match the style of the bonsai. Whether oval, round, or rectangular, the pot should be deep enough to hold sloping trunks or branches or cascade-like links that fall under the edge of the container.

Bonsai trees are wonderful works of art that have been nearby for centuries. They originally started in China and spread all over the world. Along with all the magnificent bonsai trees are the attractive pots that are occasionally explicitly made as bonsai pots. Choosing bonsai pots can help make the bonsai look good or bad. Sometimes the appearance of the bonsai has a lot to say about the plant itself; therefore, choosing the right pot for the display is crucial. Most bonsai pots are medium size and not incredibly deep. The reasons for these facts are that bonsai plants, along with the size of the pots, have a lot to say to control tree growth. Many bonsai pots have different purposes, depending on the style in which the bonsai trees are made. Other people have models that may or may not upgrade the tree. Since bonsai trees come from Asia, numerous bonsai pots have certain properties that are based on Asian models and cultures. Asian cultures usually have deep and bold colors that can sometimes be extravagant. Bonsai pots colors are generally calm and incredibly stable. The frequent colors for these pots are deep but not noticeable. The main concept of a container for bonsai trees is not to compete with the beauty of the tree, but to complement it. Bonsai pots are usually muted earth tones, which are best based on the colors of the bonsai tree planted in them. Most bonsai tree containers are usually not that deep and large. Despite these restrictions, models can still be seen in some pots. Most have Chinese or Asian species that can complement the tree in it well. Some bonsai pot models are made for certain tree species. The forest bonsai style requires a flat but sufficiently wide pot to accommodate three to seven trees. Other types of bonsai, such as a cascade or a lean, will need a pot that can be deep enough to maintain the pressure of the tree that goes down or to the side. In fact, the selection of bonsai pots for bonsai trees lies with the use of gardeners.

Here are a few factors to consider when choosing a bonsai pot or container. It is important to determine the correct size of your bonsai pot to physically keep the weight of the damp bonsai soil and support the tree. Since your bonsai tree is likely to be in an outstanding position, the last thing you want it to do is to tip over because the bonsai pot is too light or too small. So make sure your bonsai pot is big enough to carry the tree easily, but also small enough to make sure everything is balanced symmetrically. Your bonsai pot must also contain enough soil to ensure that the root system is adequately supplied with nutrients and that there is enough space for further growth. It is vital that your bonsai pot has sufficient holes in the bottom for drainage. The last thing you want is that your pot contains too much water and, therefore, over time, is likely to rot the root system of your bonsai trees. A good hint here is to use a wire mesh that fits over the drain hole. This enables proper water drainage. When it comes to this, experience and your personal aesthetics determine the right pot for your bonsai tree. If you are literally overwhelmed by the prospect of finding your own bonsai tree pot, it may be worth buying a pot specially designed for your tree. Just think about the points above, and you shouldn't be doing much wrong.

If you buy a bonsai pot or tray, you may be forgiven for the fact that an old flower pot or a plastic container will do. This is the trap that most bonsai beginners get into, and that is likely to affect your bonsai tree seriously. The art of bonsai is to replicate a naturally growing tree as closely as possible, but with one big difference, it must be miniature. It is, therefore, imperative that your bonsai pot or tray complements your bonsai tree as well as possible. When buying a bonsai pot, you should note the following: Ideally, your bonsai pot should be reserved. Keep it simple, neutral, and symmetrical, and you won't go wrong. When choosing your bonsai pot, make sure that the inner surface is not shiny or glazed. These types of pots are known to be bad for growing a bonsai tree because they can interfere with drainage, which in turn can cause many other problems. Glazed surfaces are fine on the outside; however, keep in mind that the pot is frost-proof if you keep your bonsai tree outside. Glazed pots can crack in cold weather if not previously treated. Size is also important. You need to make sure that your bonsai tree has enough room for growth. However, the pot must be small enough to provide exactly the amount of water that the tree needs. If the pot is too large, there is a risk of accidentally pouring water over your tree and rotting the roots if you leave it for a long time. Your bonsai pot must also be large enough to support the tree.

Your bonsai pot must also have enough drainage holes. Most bonsai trees prefer that the soil be kept moist at all times. Therefore, proper drainage is important when choosing a pot. Not enough drainage holes can cause your bonsai tree to get too wet, whereas too many holes can cause the soil to become too dry. It is definitely a good balancing act to do the right thing. Therefore, it is important to know how quickly your bonsai pot is running. Of course, you can buy a special bonsai pot from a specialist, and if you do that, to be honest, you can save money in the long run.

LIGHT

The appropriate amount of light for your bonsai is crucial to keep it healthy. However, there are no easy answers to how much light bonsai trees generally "need." The lighting requirements are specific to the type of tree and also depend on certain variations of the place where they are kept - namely, your home. It's a good concept to talk to your local bonsai supplier or other bonsai enthusiasts who have experience growing bonsai in an environment very similar to your own. Sunlight is by far the greatest type of light for bonsai trees and most other living things on earth. As such, the brightest window in your house is probably the best place for your indoor bonsai trees. Indoor bonsai trees moderate their growth in winter and do not require as much water, but still require sufficient humidity. Your bonsai tree needs some sunlight to grow. Each type of bonsai tree requires different amounts of sun exposure. Most bonsai thrive in full sun or partial shade on hot afternoons. Bonsai trees are often kept outdoors and although they may look small and fragile, you can be sure that they will withstand the same weather conditions as a normal-sized tree of the same variety. But in times when an extreme winter can be expected, you should take special care of your bonsai tree by isolating its roots against very cold weather. While certain tropical plants (ficus, Schefflera, etc.) can thrive indoors, most bonsai are developed from species of shrubs or trees that are adapted to the temperate climate (conifers, maple, larch, etc.) and require a period of rest. Most trees need several hours of direct or slightly filtered sun every day.

STYLE OF GROWING BONSAI

The formal upright bonsai design reproduces the growth of a tall and straight tree under favorable natural conditions. The trunk of the tree remains vertical and upright on the ground. The hull becomes smaller from the base to the tip. You may have seen some trees growing in nature with the base and apex trunk in a line perpendicular to the ground, but the growth in between is slightly inclined. Such styles are called informally upright. This is a widespread bonsai style where the plant tilts to one side, unlike the upright design we talked about. The fuselage is inclined at an angle of approximately 45 degrees to the round. The trunk can be straight or curved in this type of tree. Oblique stem plants are widespread in nature and must take this form due to the specific survival needs of the plant. One example is the sloping tree trunk that is created by searching for a source of light.

The name for bonsai in broom style comes from the shape of an inverted Japanese broom. This style matches deciduous trees and is also great for many tropical plants. In bonsai style broomsticks, the base of the trunk is straight, and the branches grow in all directions from approximately the same place on the trunk, giving it the shape of an inverted broom. This design looks elegant and represents the scene of a plant growing on the rocky slopes of a mountain. Such plants, when ripe, tend to bend down due to gravity. The plant tip goes below the root height. In the case of full cascade bonsai, the plant goes below the root level, similar to its natural counterpart. There are special pots of good height that are used for the full cascade style.

The semi-cascaded bonsai style represents a tree trunk that grows in marshy areas parallel to the water level. Here the bonsai trunk bends down, but the tip only reaches the bottom of the pot. This consists of a group of bonsai plants that are potted in such a way that they give the feeling of a mini forest.

Trees grown in this style are trained to grow upwards in a straight direction. The "sloping" bonsai is one in which the tree is either inclined to the right or left. In the cascade styles, the tree is pruned and trained to resemble a cascade waterfall. The sixth style of bonsai is known as "wind-whipped". With this style, the bonsai is trained so that it looks like it is constantly blown by the wind. The inclusion of the windswept style in the classification has given rise to some controversial breeders and traditionalists. Due to the visual interest this style can create, we considered it important to include it in a discussion of the styles of bonsai trees and be regulated by choice of style. Your choice of pot design and color will also be influenced by the type of bonsai you want to grow. To find out which type of bonsai best suits your intended design, let's take a closer look at each one. Each of these styles has some specific guidelines for that particular style. However, keep in mind that these are just guidelines. One of the most entertaining parts of the bonsai experience is creating a unique specimen. The formal post is the basis for other bonsai styles. It is a single stem that is conical in shape. With this type of bonsai, the length of the branches decreases the closer they are to the top of the tree.

BONSAI TOOLS AND TECHNIQUES

B ONSAI, LIKE ANY ART form, used specific techniques to create the masterpiece. Painters use brushes; composers use paper, pencil, and musical instruments; and sculptors use a variety of tools. Bonsai artists also use a variety of tools. The most important tools are hands, time, and patience. Bonsai has a diversity of techniques applied to this technique, such as leaf pruning, wiring, clamping, grafting, defoliation, and deadwood, to name a few. Bonsai tools are required for each of these techniques specifically for this purpose. When cutting leaves, a bonsai artist removes precise leaves or needles from the bonsai plant or tree. In this way, it contributes to the development of the mature look of the bonsai piece. The leafcutter has been specially developed for leaf removal to achieve quick, clean cuts that allow you to cut your bonsai plant/tree quickly and safely. Blunt cuts leave frayed edges that can slow healing. Tweezers are ideal for removing dead leaves as well as needles, insects, and weeds in the container. Evergreen bonsai need needles that grow on the trunk or under the distant branches. By removing new bud growth, the artist can create buds on the stem that give the bonsai character. Leaf-cutting and pruning are the two most common techniques used in bonsai creation. When trimming, branches, roots, and the trunk are removed. It is extremely important to know the advantages and disadvantages of pruning bonsai, as a wrong cut can kill or weaken a bonsai. Sharp scissors are essential for clean cuts.

Pruning, like removing leaves, is often done throughout the bonsai process. Concave cutters are the most commonly used bonsai tool for pruning branches, roots, and trunk growth. Its angled cutting edge ensures easy and clean removal of unwanted growth on your bonsai. They come in different sizes, but the standard is eight inches. Spherical, concave cutters are the sister of the concave cutters, with the only difference that they have a rounded cutting edge enabling more precise removal of the growth and allows the artist to create sacred wounds in the trunk of the bonsai, which appear flat and after healing gives the bonsai a more mature appearance. Scissors, the last of the cutting tools, have short blades with long handles. Similar to the pruning shears used in a hedge, but the size of a bonsai, they give the artist the ability to shape the bonsai and get into areas where the concave may not be able to get. To maintain the shape of the bonsai, the cut must be maintained. The time and frequency in which you need to prune depend on the type of plant or tree used. The wiring is done to shape the tree of the plant branches in the desired shape. It serves as a support and as a card into which the plant/tree is inserted. Copper and aluminum wire is used for wiring branches or trunks of the bonsai. The wire remains in place for up to nine months or until the branch hardens. Cables are also used to form shapes with young branches that are still flexible or to connect them to the bonsai pot. Due to the lack of flexibility, not all industries are responsible for the cabling. These branches are shaped by trimming and brought into the desired positions. Wiring is most common in spring when there is new growth, and the branches are more flexible. When wiring, you should take special care not to slow down or bark the branches too much. Hold the wire firmly and in difficult places (e.g. bends, crossovers) to reach the goal to be reached. The most common tool for wiring your bonsai is the wire cutter.

A bonsai artist not only cuts the wire with the wire cutters but often forms the end of the cable tightly around the branches. The bonsai cable cutters have a rounded nose that allows the artist to approach the branch and not damage the bark. Branch benders are used instead of the wire if the branches are not flexible enough to wire in the desired positions. Tensioning is another technique with which the bonsai artist forms branches and trunks that present stiffer wood. Screw clamps are most commonly used to allow the artist to apply pressure to the branch or trunk over a long period of time to achieve the desired results. The grafting is done to connect two plants or trees to give the appearance of a unique bonsai. Another common reason for grafting is that some plant root systems cannot stand alone in bonsai art. The combination of the two root systems gives the artist better control over the size. Common tools used in grafting are propagating and budding knives. The artist needs to use sharp knives to avoid leaving ragged wounds that can damage the bonsai. Binding and wrapping materials are used to hold cracks and supplies together and prevent a callus from forming. Frequently used binding and packaging materials are adhesive tape, plastic, bast, rubber bud strips, and cord. Defoliation is the practice of complete leaf removal by partially cutting off along the petiole (stem) of the leaf, which will later dry out and fall off. This forces a new form of smaller leaves, which enhances the aesthetics of said dwarfism. This brief dwarf growth of the leaves can occur at most every two years due to the debilitating effect on the tree. Not all plants/trees can survive defoliation. Sharp bonsai scissors are the most habitual tool for this technique. Deadwooding is a technique used to give an otherwise young tree the appearance of a ripened bark. There are two different types of deadwood processing. The jin used when the bark is completely removed from a branch and the shari technique when trying to give the impression of scars on a branch or trunk. Other techniques are used to give the appearance of a raised grain in a stem or to bleach the stem using a lime-sulfur compound. There are many other techniques used in bonsai art and a variety of different tools to achieve the effect of the technique.

There are very few guidelines regarding weird bonsai. First of all, the first branch has to spread in the opposite direction of the slope. The other rule is that the top of the tree should be facing the front or side of the tree. This bonsai style is a compromise between the upright style and the cascade style. An important difference between the sloping bonsai and the cascading bonsai is that the tree grows above the root line in the sloping bonsai, whereas the growth in the cascade styles occurs below the root line. Except for the fruit-bearing trees, almost every other tree could be trained in this style. There are two classifications within the cascade style of bonsai plants, the "Cascade Bonsai" and the "Semi Cascade Bonsai". These trees are instructed so that the trunk of the tree grows straight up and then turns drastically down to the bottom of the tree. The distinction between the cascade and the semi-cascade is the direction in which growth takes place. In the cascade, the tree continues to grow vertically to the earth, whereas the semi-cascade eventually begins to grow horizontally. This horizontal growth always takes place under the base of the tree. In both species, the main part of tree growth takes place under the base of the tree. This growth extends beyond the bottom of the pot that contains the Cascade bonsai. For this reason, Cascade Bonsai are usually placed either on a high table or on a pedestal. A good choice for one of these styles would be juniper, chrysanthemum, wisteria, willow, and star jasmine. You wouldn't choose a tree that is naturally a high growth product to style as a cascade bonsai. These trees come into their own best when planted in a round or hexagonal pot. The pot for the cascading bonsai should constantly be much larger than they are wide. As with other bonsai trees, this style shows best when planted off-center.

The final grouping of styles for the bonsai tree is known as "Windswept Bonsai". What distinguishes this style from the others is the visual hardness of the presentation. As the name suggests, the "Windswept Bonsai" has the appearance of a tree that has grown in extremely harsh conditions, with winds or other environmental conditions forcing growth on only one side of the tree, typically facing away from the wind. In this type of bonsai, everything including the trunk, branches, and the leaves point in one direction. The wind-swept bonsai is not to be confused with the sloping bonsai. Both styles have a curved or angled trunk, but the slope and branches can return to the trunk. With a wind-swept bonsai, there is no change of direction. A wind-swept bonsai usually has a stunted or weathered appearance.

There will be little or no decoration in the pot. Keep in mind that the goal is to create a presentation that reflects the toughest conditions. This tree is usually planted in an oval pot, with the tree itself being planted towards an edge of the pot. The growth is again towards the center of the pot. To define the harsh conditions, you can add stones to the presentation. Remember to keep the rocks the right size of the tree. If these trees occur in nature, they are very mature, large trees. So don't reduce their size if the rocks are too big. Wind-swept bonsai are usually grown from evergreen plants. The use of deciduous trees is not advised for this type of bonsai. While the deciduous trees could be trained in a wind-swept style, the fact that their leaves grow in all directions would make the visual effect less convincing. Wind-swept bonsai is usually filled into simple, unadorned pots. The use of glazed or colored pots would affect the overall presentation. If you were looking for a single word to describe the appearance of "Windswept Bonsai," that single word would be "survivor". While this design may not be as visually fulfilling, it is definitely one of the most dramatic styles. Learning bonsai-growing has many wonderful benefits. That's why it's part of the challenge to learn how to properly care for and train the trees and keep them healthy and alive for many years!

HOW TO PRUNE AND GROW BONSAI TREES

Growing a bonsai tree is very different from growing a maple tree in your garden. Plant, feed, and water the tree with the maple tree. And aside from occasional pruning to remove dead or damaged branches, just sit back and let nature take control. With a bonsai, however, you grow a specimen with a defined "appearance" from day one. You will trim and train the tree to achieve this look. Nature can make the tree grow, but you determine its final appearance. While the final look of the tree is part of the grower's interpretation, there are five or six defined styles that your bonsai fall into. Within the first five designations, you will find the "Formal Upright" bonsai, the "Informal Upright" bonsai, the "Slanting" bonsai, the "Cascade" bonsai and the "Semi Cascade" bonsai. Growing bonsai from seeds is the longest route to your own bonsai. We believe that it is also the most rewarding because you can see every step of the way. When growing a seed bonsai, you need to consider which species you want to grow. If you choose an outdoor tree, you need to consider the "stratification time". If the type you choose needs a winter period to sleep, the seed will need it to germinate. This process, in which we usually put the seed in the fridge or in peat moss to simulate winter, is called layering the seed. You can also plant and leave the seeds outdoors during the fall, but you will have a much lower success rate this way. After this process, the seed can be planted for growing in soil. Wait for the recommended time to germinate and water as needed without going overboard. Water when the surface of the floor looks dry, and use an air dome if possible. Once your semen sprouts, we recommend that you spray it with some antifungal to increase your chances of survival. Continue pouring and transplanting into a larger container after seeing your first "real leaves". Let your bonsai grow as usual, following our guide to your species until it becomes a pre-bonsai. You can grow your seeds into pre-bonsai or skip this step and buy a tree at this stage.

A houseplant suffers from the dryness caused by heating or air conditioning. You may need to buy a humidifier or place water bowls near your bonsai to be happy. Some suitable indoor types are Fukien tea, Hawaiian umbrella tree, bush cherry, and starflower. Outdoor bonsai range from black pine and other conifers to maple and Chinese elm. When you buy a bonsai, you also need special tools and consumables to shape it and keep it healthy. You don't have to buy a special bonsai fertilizer, but you want plant food that also contains nitrogen, phosphorus, and potassium. You'll also need high-quality tools, including long-handled scissors to prune branches, smaller scissors to trim buds, shoots, and roots, and a root rake or hook to untangle the root balls when potting the tree again. Anodized copper wire is required for your tree to grow in a certain shape. If you want to pot a bonsai tree from scratch, there are several methods needed for propagation to consider. Growing from seeds is fairly easy, but it will take a few years for a plant to mature enough to form a bonsai. Growing seedlings or planting cuttings from other plants are not difficult, and you will have to work with them a little earlier. Bonsai are trained in one of several traditional styles designed to mimic the natural shape of a tree, for example: when the wind is blowing or when you reach up towards the sun. These forms - formal upright, informal upright, slope, cascade, and broom - are achieved by wiring the branches of the tree. The wire is bent to lure the branch in the desired direction as it grows. The wires are preserved for a full growing season, and the trees can be rewired in the following growing periods as needed. If you properly care for a bonsai indoors or outdoors, you need to provide your tree with the appropriate amount of sunlight, water, and food. Over-watering is a common mistake. The soil should always be moist, but never be soupy or completely dry. Once you see the roots of your bonsai circling the bottom of the container, you need to repot it. Choosing a bonsai pot is part of the art of bonsai. Bonsai experts choose containers that artistically compliment their trees. Glazed, colorful pots work best for tropical, flowering bonsai unglazed, earth-colored pots go well with most outdoor bonsai varieties, such as pine. It is also crucial that the size and shape of the pot match the style and height of the tree.

If you are interested enough to develop bonsai trees, some simple guidelines can help you carry out the activity. Note that a bonsai, even if it's a miniature thing, needs more care and maintenance. To cultivate bonsai trees, you should buy seedlings that are specifically designed to become bonsai. There are also wood shavings that could be turned into a beautiful bonsai. You couldn't just turn a pruning or seedling into a bonsai. You need to use bonsai soil to expand bonsai trees. It should be potted. Bonsai soil is sold in plant houses or in botanical shops. This type of soil dries out much faster than the usual type of soil, perfect for bonsai that constantly need water but don't want to be over-sucked. Adequate humidity is required to grow bonsai trees. Place the bonsai pot in a tray with shallow water. This way, the tree could easily feel the moisture around it.

When growing bonsai trees, you need to prune the tree at certain times of the year. Pruning bonsai trees is the job of peeling the old and rotted bark on the trunk or easily maintaining the top appearance and even the root portion of the bonsai. When pruning bonsai trees, you should prune your bonsai carefully in spring or autumn. That means you have to trim the tree at least once a year. When pruning bonsai trees remove any unnecessary branches that sprout in the trunk, that will help preserve the beauty and artistic value of your bonsai. You don't want your bonsai to look cluttered and messy, do you? Concentrate equally on the ground and the roots of the tree. When trimming the stem and leaves, you are also trimming the roots. Cut off the roots if you want the growth to be neutralized and balanced. When growing bonsai trees, you need to prune your bonsai regularly. Pruning bonsai trees help keep the desired shape and size of the tree.

Now you know that keeping a bonsai is like having a pet at home. Bonsai are mostly outdoor plants and should be kept outdoors all year round. That doesn't mean, of course, that they can't come in for a short time, just that they have to be outside most of the time. Bonsai enjoy temperate climates that give them rest. Dormancy is a survival strategy that plants in temperate climates have developed to stay alive through the winter. These plants have an internal clock that tells them when to slow down their growth activity so that they can survive extreme or frozen temperatures. For the local bonsai artist, you need an outdoor space where your plants are kept.

Bonsai are trained to look different using different techniques. This can be accomplished by manipulating the trunk and branches by pruning and wiring. Here lies the heart of bonsai art. Errors in this training area can lead to fatal results. But don't be discouraged. Anyone with enough training and time can learn how to train their bonsai properly. There are many different bonsai techniques for propagating bonsai trees. The most natural way to propagate bonsai is by seeds. This is a very slow process and is generally suitable for growing bonsai. Growing bonsai from seeds would take longer, but it also gives you more control over how to get the bonsai into the shape you want. The trunk of the bonsai tree can be shaped in the early years, and this would make it much easier for the bonsai artist to shape it according to the design. The germination process of the seeds usually takes one to two years or more, depending on the plant variety. With some bonsai techniques like cold layering, you can speed up the germination process. For the experienced bonsai grower, grafting is one of the other options for propagating bonsai trees. Most bonsai experts prefer to perform split or whip transplants in winter or in the early spring seasons. One of the other techniques for propagation is cutting. It is definitely faster to grow bonsai by pruning than from seeds. If you plan to grow your bonsai by pruning, plan to start it in late spring or early summer.

The other most common bonsai technique used to grow new bonsai trees is to layer them in the air from an existing plant. This method gives you a bonsai with the most developed root system. Choose a branch from your existing bonsai plant that is in good shape and shape and cut the branch at an angle. Cover the cut with a soil made up of a good mixture of organic and inorganic components. Water the soil for about eight to nine months, and by then, some good root development should develop from the cut part of the plant. Once you have balanced root development, you can cut off the entire branch from where roots started and create a new bonsai from it. Make sure the parent plant is in a healthy state before you air your bonsai trees. Another advantage of air stratification is that multiple branches of the same tree can be stratified at the same time.

One of the hallmarks of the formal erector is the position of the first branch. This first branch should appear at 1/3 of the trunk height; it should also point to the front of the tree. The second arm should also be trained to point to the front of the tree. A third branch should protrude from the trunk. This third branch should appear at an angle halfway between the first and second branches. Subsequent branches should pursue this pattern to the top of the tree. The final appearance of the tree should be roughly a triangle. When growing a formal upright bonsai, do not center the plant in the pot. This placement is for visual purposes only. Formal upright bonsai look best in an oval or rectangular pot. Keep away square pots, as this affects the appearance of the tree. The formal post is one of the easiest shapes to create. Recommended plants that work well for formal upright bonsai are pine, maple, juniper, and larch. It is recommended to avoid fruit trees for the formally upright style.

The informal upright bonsai is a single stem that is planted in a pot, just like the formal upright bonsai. The placement or position of the branches as they originate from the trunk follows the same procedural logic as informal uprightness. Apart from these two provisions, the informal upright bonsai and the formal upright bonsai are two very different plants. In the Informal Upright Bonsai, the trunk of the tree is not necessarily straight. It can even bend or rotate several times before it reaches its apex. A properly trained informal stem bonsai will bend forward or to the visible side of the tree when it reaches its apex. The branches in a bonsai with an informal stem appear to be fuller than in a bonsai with Fukien tea. There is less symmetry with informal upright than with formal upright. As with formal upright bonsai, pine, maple, and juniper are also good choices for informal upright bonsai. Avoid fruit trees for this design.

Informal upright bonsai appear best when planted in either an oval or rectangular pot. If you are potting an informal upright bonsai, plant it off-center in your pot. If your chosen plant has no significant bend or slope, just adjust the angle of the root ball when you plant the sample. When visiting your local kindergarten, you should be able to fell several trees that already have a natural bend or twist on the trucks, making them the ideal choice for this bonsai style. The sloping bonsai tree has a very steep or acute angle compared to the two previous styles, which have been discussed. While the trunk of the tree grows vertically in the upright forms, the trunk of the sloping tree leans drastically in one direction. The angle at which the tree grows is between 60 and 80 degrees. Sloping bonsai trees are often found in nature, where the tree had to bend in one direction to locate the sun or where the prevailing wind kept pushing the tree in one direction. The sloping bonsai is a miniature version of the same tree. Bonsai art migrated from China to Japan, where it was first worshiped by monastic societies, noble houses, and finally, by ordinary people. The western world discovered bonsai after World War II, and today there are bonsai societies and enthusiasts around the world.

If you have decided to start growing bonsai trees, the first thing you should do is figure out which life cycle phase of the tree you want to start with. Bonsai can be grown either from seeds, from bonsai nurseries, from layers of earth or from cuttings. If you're just establishing out, you should probably stick to growing your tree from cuttings.

The earlier you start the bonsai development cycle, the more difficult it will be to keep the bonsai tree alive. Keep in mind that when you start sowing, you need to create an ideal environment for the bonsai to live in. Starting from cuttings will, therefore, be less difficult since the bonsai has already passed the crucial phase of its own life cycle. But why don't we take a closer look at each strategy? It doesn't necessarily mean that you can't have a very nice bonsai, even though you start from the seed.

1.) Develop bonsai from cuttings

For bonsai beginners, this is certainly the easiest way, unless you want to buy a finished bonsai in the bonsai nursery. The good thing about this particular option is that the most critical phase of bonsai growing has ended. In addition, pruning the tree is less difficult since the cuttings now indicate how the tree wants to grow. Even so, it is too much time for many people to wait for the tree from cuttings to develop to its full beauty, and instead, they decide to buy a finished bonsai. It can take up to 2 years before you get your first bonsai.

2.) Growing bonsai from layering

Another choice, similar to the first one, is to grow bonsai from layers of soil or air. This method requires a shorter time for your bonsai to reach its full potential. During this phase, it is possible to see already the tree structure, so cutting unnecessary branches is an easy task.

3.) Bonsai tree from seeds

Just like becoming a parent and seeing your child grow from the very first moment, growing seeds from bonsai could be a similar experience in away. Quite a few experienced bonsai tree designers choose this option because it works best for them. Remember that it can take up to 4 years for your bonsai to be in the same shape as they were bought in a shop. If you're a newbie, your bonsai may not make it if you don't create excellent conditions from the start. Whichever alternative you choose, you will have a lot of fun seeing how your little tree develops and matures.

THE DIFFERENCES BETWEEN INDOOR AND OUTDOOR BONSAI TREES

HERE ARE TWO FUNDAMENTAL differences in the world of the bonsai tree: the bonsai is either an indoor or an outdoor bonsai. Bonsai trees are essentially

miniaturized trees that were created in this way by the forces of nature for the wild varieties of bonsai, or that were intentionally made in this way by regular and specific pruning of the crown and roots. The size of these miniature trees also depends on the size of the container in which they are grown, as the size of their roots is constantly controlled. The plants used for bonsai are usually trees, but most larger shrubs and plants can also be used to make bonsai plants. A common mistake among bonsai growers is that they wait too long to start shaping their bonsai trees. Most professional growers and many books recommend that you shape your tree after the initial growth phase. And from a gardening point of view, that is correct, but from a practical point of view, it is far too late. The shape of your bonsai tree should actually start before you buy the tree. The first step in designing your bonsai begins with a plan. Determine how your adult tree should look. Think about how sparse or sparse bonsai should appear. Do you want the bonsai to create a special emotion, or do you simply rely on the natural beauty of the tree? A matured bonsai plan helps us make an informed decision about the type of bonsai that will help us achieve our plan. If your plan includes a single stately tree with very delicate leaves, a moderate bonsai like the maple tree may be ideal for you. Or if your plan is more tropical, a member of the tropical bonsai family may work better for you.

Part of this plan should also incorporate where you plan to grow the bonsai indoors or outdoors. Along with this information, the plan should also consider the part of the world you live in. Some areas of the world are not compatible with all types of bonsai. For example, a tropical bonsai can be damaged by frost, while a temperate bonsai can withstand milder temperatures. The bonsai tree is shaped by pruning to remove excess branches and leaves. Once removed, the branches are often trained to grow in a particular direction using small wires that guide the branches. But without a plan and the right bonsai, it is almost impossible to get the bonsai that we all see in our thoughts.

Bonsai trees are indeed wonderful works of art and, in many cases, have been manipulated to simulate some animals or figures. These bonsai trees are usually arranged as either outdoor bonsai trees or indoor bonsai trees. The outdoor bonsai variety usually tolerates a cold winter. In contrast, the indoor bonsai trees usually come from the tropics and need to be kept in a similar climate, which is why they are used indoors. They can be beautiful focal points in homes or offices and can easily be viewed as decorative works of art. Larger trees can be used for bonsai planting, but some are recommended or more suitable for beginners simply because they grow reasonably easily and do not die easily. They are the schefflera, sago palms, aralia, gardenias, serissa, fucia tea, bougainvillea, bush cherry, including some types of elms. These trees are the ideal indoor bonsai trees for bonsai enthusiasts or beginners. Some other bonsai trees may be better suited for outdoor growing, mainly due to some factors that influence the plants in some way, such as the need to throw leaves in winter. The indoor bonsai trees, which are ideal for indoor use, come from the tropical and subtropical regions, so they need the morning and afternoon sun. It is of the utmost importance to ensure that they are sufficiently exposed even in enclosed spaces so that they grow evenly and steadily.

These particular varieties of indoor bonsai trees are unlikely to work as well if they are exposed to the cold in winter (if grown in cold and temperate regions) because they come from the tropics. If they are exposed to cold winter weather, they can easily die. It is common comprehension that most indoor bonsai trees can be treated as well as most houseplants; after all, they are houseplants. Likewise, it is most often necessary to water only when the soil in the pots feels dry. They should also often be exposed to late or early sunlight. The use of fluorescent and incandescent lamps should be enough to meet this need for some indoor bonsai trees. With hope, many people are very interested in taking up the hobby of growing miniature bonsai trees indoors, simply and for decoration purposes. However, some people prefer to grow their hobby outdoors bonsai trees as they tend to find this activity more attractive. In fact, there is not much of a difference between the indoor and outdoor bonsai trees, and the style is pretty much the same. However, what differentiates them is the larger scale and the difference in the environment in which they grow. In fact, there are two specimens of outdoor bonsai trees, namely the evergreens (like juniper and pine) and deciduous trees (like oak), which lose their leaves in autumn or autumn and reproduce in spring. The ability to pot them in pots outdoors makes them an easy choice for many.

OUTDOOR BONSAI PLANT

Another characteristic of outdoor bonsai trees is their inability to grow indoors for long periods, despite needing to be inside so they do not freeze even in the cold, winter months. In addition to the need to properly water and maintain bonsai trees outdoors, this is a very important aspect that must be followed closely. Many beginners can be easily fooled by the appearance of the topsoil, which looks dry but actually still contains moisture. Once the bonsai trees are planted outdoors, it's important to keep an eye on the water level. To do this, you need to stick your fingers into the ground at a depth of about an inch to determine how much moisture the soil really contains. Dry soil is not allowed, and it is a requirement that you water it thoroughly immediately, while you may need to measure the water level every two weeks. This should be enough to ensure that the soil contains enough moisture. During the winter months, you can relax in the irrigation periods. However, you should have the assurance that you only water when the temperature is at least forty-five degrees or more. When caring for your bonsai trees outdoors, it is also important to note that your trees need to be fertilized. Depending on the brand of fertilizer used, the amount and frequency should be sufficient to ensure that the growth of the trees is maintained in accordance with the recommended standards. If you fertilize every 14 days, this should be enough to keep your trees within the growth parameters. However, also note that fertilization in winter is a big no. The category of fertilizer to be used does not make much of a difference for most tree species, but the use of liquid fertilizer on the foliage can be considered by most to be the ideal leveling measure during the fertilization process. Apart from the need to fertilize the ground of the bonsai trees outdoors, it is also necessary to prune and cut the trees with special tree cutters or sharp pruning shears, and this must always be taken into account. Careful care and maintenance of your bonsai trees should be considered, as this will help improve the health and appearance of your bonsai trees outdoors. By following these simple tips and advice, you should make sure that you enjoy your hobby and have fun caring for your outdoor bonsai trees as they grow to reach their full potential.

Outdoor bonsai, known as temperate bonsai, thrive in the colder climates of the world, while indoor or tropical bonsai, as they are called, cannot survive the cold. If you decide to grow an indoor bonsai, there are some peculiarities to consider. Indoor bonsai are like all other trees because they need enough light to grow. The lack of adequate lighting is one of the main reasons that indoor bonsai do not grow. Your indoor bonsai should be placed near a window. A recommendation is that you turn your bonsai tree regularly, as it is a natural tendency for the tree to find the light source. Rotation is important even if you want the tree to grow in a certain direction. The lack of even light across the entire tree can hinder its growth. Depending on the local temperature and humidity, your indoor bonsai should be placed outdoors during the summer months. However, keep an eye on them and bring them back to the house or put them in a shady place when temperatures get extreme. If you don't have an aperture where you can place the indoor bonsai, you can simulate natural sunlight with special fluorescent lamps. These lamps are called Grow-Lux lamps. These lamps should be placed within 6 inches of your system. The Grow-Lux lamps can be installed in almost any fluorescent lamp. In the winter months, it is prudent to use these lamps at least twelve hours a day. As with most plants, water is a crucial element for plant survival. The bottom of the bonsai tree should always be kept moist unless you plan to prune or wire the tree. The floor should be dry at these two times. Once you have completed the wiring or the cut, you should water the bonsai and let it bounce back. Outside of these special times, you can check the moisture content of the floor by either scratching the surface with your finger or by inserting a stick into the floor. When watering the bonsai, remember to water the bonsai from above, not the roots. The last thing to understand is that the bonsai must be fertilized. Follow the schedule recommended by the manufacturer. Over-fertilization is almost the worst than under-fertilization.

INDOOR BONSAI PLANTS

Indoor bonsai care can be a fairly difficult process, to say the least. Without proper care and attention, bonsai trees are prone to dying, which is rather unfortunate for the grower and the tree itself. Many people have different views on how to properly care for bonsai trees. In a way, caring for indoor bonsai is similar to building a house - you need solid foundations before you can finish the rest of the building. You should place your bonsai in a place that gets plenty of sunlight (the window is a natural choice for most, but make sure the windowsill is wide enough to hold the pot properly, so it doesn't accidentally fall over) the room is neither too warm nor too cold (room climat works well if the tree has a good light source, but this can vary from species to species). Also, make sure that the room is sufficiently humid so that the floor doesn't dry out too quickly. Indoor bonsai tree varieties. What follows is a list of popular indoor bonsai trees: Fukien tea tree (Carmona macrophylle), Chinese elm (Ulmusparvifolia), Chinese snow rose or Serissa (Serissafoetida or Serissa japonica), Chinese pepper (Zanthoxylumpiperitum), Chinese plum (Sageteriatheezans), Jade baby (Crassulaportulacea), Willow leaf fig or narrow leaf (Ficussalicifolia), Bougainville (Bougainvillea) or paper flower, Lucky tree or money tree (Pachiraaquatica), Buddhist pine (Podocarpus Chinese yew), Chinese privet (Ligustrumnitida), Sacred Bamboo (Nandinadomestica). The other variety of bonsai is known as outdoor bonsai. These bonsai prefer an open environment and can be divided into two main categories, foliage, and evergreen. The outdoor bonsai also need proper care and nutrients to stay healthy and grow beautifully. The deciduous bonsai sheds its leaves in autumn and hibernates in winter. New leaves appear in spring. The Evergreen Bonsai, however, keeps its leaves in all seasons. In winter, however, the plant is in a resting phase, in which its leaves usually change to a dull green or yellowish color. Variety of Bonsai Tree Outdoor is foliage plants, maple, ginkgo, Elms, larch, ornamental, apricot, hornbeam, Evergreen plants, juniper, Pine trees, boxwood, azaleas.

By growing bonsai indoors, you can control the growth environment of your plants. Indoor temperatures can be easily controlled. This way, you can grow bonsai that normally doesn't grow in your region. Loving bonsai trees can also be grown indoors. The humidity can also be kept under control. Bonsai are temperamental plants and prefer moist air. You can keep the humidity at the level that the plants like. You can also ensure that your bonsai tree is properly lit. If you leave it outside, the lighting depends on the sunshine. By growing bonsai indoors, you can create natural light with artificial sunlight that allows for better and more even growth. The irrigation of the plants is also easier to control inside. You can water your plants easily when needed without fear of watering too much. The soil can be monitored to ensure that it is kept at the level of moisture that the bonsai likes.

By growing your bonsai indoors, you can enjoy your

hobby all year round. You can watch your plants at any time.

The plants thrive in a controlled climate in which they can grow. Caring for your plants is much easier if you monitor your plants daily. You can immediately identify and correct any problems that arise. By keeping your bonsai plants inside, you can also eliminate many of the pest problems that can arise when growing bonsai outdoors. Bonsai plants help decorate your home. You can also grow all kinds of bonsai plants. You no longer have to rely on the temperatures in your area to determine which plants to grow. Indoor cultivation allows you to pick from hundreds of bonsai trees. If you have a bonsai tree in the house, nature comes into the house.

GUIDELINE TO HELP YOU PURCHASE THE BEST BONSAI TREE

CHOOSING THE BEST BONSAI tree is straightforward. Pick a bonsai based on your experience in growing bonsai. If you are a beginner or are buying as a gift,

you should choose an easy-care bonsai tree at a reasonable price. Although many indoor bonsai trees say "carefree," you still need to water and keep growing every day. Jump into more difficult bonsais with increasing experience. When I chose my first bonsai, I didn't read much about growing bonsai. There are a few things to observe when selecting your first bonsai tree. Given that killing them is a little more difficult starting with a carefree bonsai is ideal. I also started with a few tools to train and prune trees and plants. Once you've mastered a few techniques, you should head to bonsai trees, which require a little more patience. You also want to think about your climate zone when choosing your bonsai. If you live in the south, you should have little or no freezing. If so, many indoor trees can be great outdoors all year round. Just make sure you read what the tree can handle before you bring it inside. Just because you don't live in a climate zone that's warm all year round doesn't mean you can't have tropical bonsai. If you have a bright area (windowsill, skylight, or even growing light), you should be sure that you can take care of your bonsai. Although you can use a bonsai light to give your bonsai trees some light, I would recommend placing them in a well-lit place from time to time. There is nothing better than good sunshine. Another right choice when choosing a bonsai tree is the outdoor bonsai. These trees need a rest period in winter. Some of the outdoor bonsai lose their foliage in winter, as does the tree itself, while others are evergreen. If you choose an outdoor bonsai, you should always think about the level of experience. If you have no experience, you want to start with an easy-care bonsai. Since a bonsai tree grows in an unnatural environment, you need to make sure that you provide it with all it needs to thrive. The bonsai care instructions require the right soil conditions, adequate irrigation, feeding, and training.

The word "wa" in Japanese means "harmony" and is the relationship between nature and man. However, it can also mean a work of art. In bonsai or bonsai art, this concept is about finding a balance between the type of tree used, the style that is pruned or shaped, and the container or pot in which the bonsai tree lives. The bonsai pot or container is a fundamental aspect of bonsai art and should be given due consideration. The material used color, and of course, the size and shape must be researched when a bonsai tree is married into a pot or container. There are no really strict rules here, as your decision is likely due to your personal preferences. However, it is a good point to keep the bonsai art tradition and ensure that your pot has a sense of symmetry and, above all, complements your bonsai tree and is more likely to be pleasing to the eye.

When choosing a bonsai tree, you will find that a variety of species are available. Bonsai trees have many types, such as cascade, formal, upright, raft, and literati. Their size may vary depending on the type of tree you have selected. They come in various sizes, such as miniature, small, and average. Some trees can be small fruits or flowers. When choosing a bonsai tree, you should also consider whether to keep it indoors or outdoors. If you just want a tree that is easy to care for, that would be an indoor bonsai. They can be about as easy to care for as your houseplants. Indoor bonsai trees are tropical and subtropical. These trees need to be placed in a place where morning sunlight and afternoon shade. Some types of bonsai work well in full sunlight. If you plan to set up your bonsai tree outdoors in the summer, be careful not to let it stand at temperatures below fifty-five degrees. Trees suitable for beginners can be a baby jade or a Hawaiian umbrella, just mention a few of the trees you need to choose from. Bonsai is also available in other varieties such as cherry trees, Fukien tea aralias, elms, and bougainvilleas.

When looking for an outdoor tree, you can choose from certain evergreen trees such as juniper, pine, elm, ginkgo, and maple. These trees are attractive all year round. Some of the evergreen trees are called boxwood, pine, and azalea juniper. A popular type that is popular with people is the juniper tree with its beautiful appearance. Evergreen bonsai need proper care to look good. Some of the many varieties of bonsai are hornbeam, maple, crab apple, elm, larch, and apricot. Japanese maples can be a more difficult tree to grow. They are famous for their colorful foliage with bright red, yellow, and orange colors throughout the year. The different types of bonsai should be looked after very carefully, especially in the cold months of the year. They need to be protected during the year when the temperature drops outdoors. People love indoor bonsai because they are so big and can grow indoors. Regardless of the type of bonsai tree you choose, you are in a class of its own.

HOW TO DEVELOP A BONSAI

There are several ways to develop bonsai. Bonsai can be grown from seeds or cuttings, from young trees or from naturally occurring stunted trees that have been planted in containers. Most bonsai are between one and five meters high. Bonsai are kept small and developed by pruning branches and roots, repotting them at regular intervals, pinching off new widening, and wiring the branches and trunk so that they take on the desired shape.

Bonsai are normal trees or plants, not special hybrid dwarfs. Small-leaved varieties work best, but basically, any plant can be used, regardless of the size to which it grows in the wild. The bonsai may suggest many things, but they must always look natural and never show human hands, except for the Chinese bonsai, which in many cases represent images of dragons and other influential symbols of culture at the time of their creation. Grown in special containers, bonsai are mostly grown outdoors (except some indoor plants that are designed, grown, and grown), although they are often exhibited indoors on special occasions. The bonsai, with its container and soil, is physically independent of the earth, since its roots are not planted in it, a separate entity that is complete in itself and yet part of nature. A bonsai tree should always be placed off-center in its container, because not only the asymmetry is decisive for the visual effect, but the center is also symbolic where heaven and earth meet, and nothing should take this place.

LEARN ADVANCED BONSAI TECHNIQUES

If you learn advanced bonsai techniques, you can develop unique shapes and appearances for your trees and plants. These types of methods may require additional skills, labor, and maintenance to get these types of horticultural masterpieces. No question performing a "root-over-rock" style or creating a "broom" style is more advanced bonsai techniques. However, the question may be whether the tree or plant can survive the transformation if less experienced people do this. It takes a lot of patience to see the results of the advanced bonsai techniques. Even exotic seed germination, creating a natural deadwood effect, or releasing wood rot can be problems for the more demanding bonsai grower. Whether you need to know how to take care of your bonsai, or just know how to plant bonsai trees differently, it is important to understand how learning advanced bonsai techniques affect your bottom line.

Learning advanced bonsai techniques range from bending branches with bast to learning techniques for refining threads. Trunk tapering and the creation of new branches are among the artistic principles of bonsai. Developing your own bonsai tree from a root seedling can be considered part of the usual bonsai techniques, but splitting the trunk to heal the inverse rejuvenation can be considered one of the more advanced bonsai techniques. Whether you're cutting, wiring, styling, or repotting, you can always learn more about the ancient Japanese art of bonsai.

One of the special features of bonsai is miniaturization with life-size replicas. Other special features may include wines, exposed root styles, and driftwood or literary style bonsai.

Viewing multiple bonsai trees in a forest or raft style can be considered as an advanced bonsai technique that will add artistic interest to your collection.

Displaying a bonsai tree can affect the aesthetic value of your horticultural composition, but with good proportions and balance, even the simplest techniques can achieve excellent results. For those who are just kicking off to explore the more complicated methods of growing bonsai trees, the basics can be important, but still be expanded. If you want to learn advanced bonsai techniques, you may need to learn the basics and experiment with different styles and improvements. Growing bonsai can produce beautiful art projects if appropriately done with unique growing methods.

DESIGN YOUR BONSAI PLANT FOR HEALTH AND BEAUTY

A bonsai is a miniature replica of a natural tree. It is a combination of art and nature that fascinates and delights anyone who has had the privilege of seeing a magnificent specimen of a tree in bonsai. As an art form, the shape of a bonsai plant is required for the appearance of a natural tree. But did you know that the shape and cut are also necessary for the health of the plant? Historically, if you wanted to shape a bonsai, you used weights attached to branches or tied branches to the bottom or bottom of the pot with a string. However, with the development of technology and manufacturing techniques, it has become standard to form a bonsai tree with wire. When shaping a bonsai plant, consider the natural shape and slope of the tree before you start. When it grows tall and straight, you don't want to try to train it to grow in a cascade style. You also don't want to try to prepare a willow that naturally evolves into a formal upright style in crying style. Consider the mainline. Shaping a bonsai is more about guiding it along with its natural inclinations than forcing it into a mechanical shape. Bonsai is the connection between art and nature, and they have to work in harmony to work well. Once you've decided on a general shape for your bonsai, it's important to choose the right type of wire. You want to make sure you take a wire that won't damage the trunk, branches, or bottom of the bonsai. Some people use copper wire, but as copper becomes more expensive and harmful chemicals can get into the floor, aluminum wire or plastic-coated wire has become increasingly popular.

When molding your bonsai plant, make sure that you haven't watered it for at least a day. A freshly watered bonsai tree has branches that are too stiff to shape well. Doing so can damage your plant. Ideally, you should shape your bonsai tree in early spring just before the growing season. This trains your small tree so that it grows in the desired shape. Be careful not to over-wire a bonsai tree, as this can scar the trunk or branches and prevent the sap from flowing into the tree. When wiring, start with the thickest part of the trunk or branch and work carefully to the thinnest part. Be careful not to enfold the wire too tightly together, as this has little effect on the shape. Make sure your wiring gently guides your tree into the shape you want. It generally takes an entire growing season to shape your bonsai tree after wiring. However, if it has not yet been shaped to your satisfaction, always remove the wire at the end of the growing season and rewire it if you intend to continue developing your bonsai tree for a second season. This will avoid marks and scars on your bonsai tree. "As the branch is bent, the tree is inclined" is a wonderful and valid principle that you have to follow when shaping your bonsai.

The art of making bonsai is enhanced by the many different ways in which you can manipulate your bonsai tree. You will find numerous species that you can make with your bonsai and that are offered for viewing in every bonsai gallery. You may not know the names of the different types of bonsai in a bonsai gallery, but you will find out soon. This fashion is widely used in bonsai galleries. The overall effect of your bonsai tree is that you have a straight, upward-growing tree, the tip of which has a visible taper. Visible rejuvenation is usually a necessity observed in every bonsai gallery to showcase fashion. The trunk floor with the miniature tree must be defined so thick that it tapers towards the top. Upright fashion has many different subspecies that can be seen in every bonsai gallery. Another typical design found in a bonsai gallery is the crooked design. It is also referred to as wind sweeping or slanting style because it gives the impression that the tree was forced to lean on a particular path due to the strong wind, or because the sun dominated on a path. As you may see in a bonsai gallery, there are also numerous rules that determine whether a bonsai really differs from the weird design. This includes that the initial branch takes the opposite path of the slope from the bonsai tree and that the roots are placed in good condition directly under the slope.

This is usually a fairly common way that takes some work on your serving to maintain. Some bonsai gallery tours show this type of fashion because it shows how a tree can grow down instead of the traditional post. There are several sub-styles that fall under this design. This shows a tree growing on the side of a mountain that has limited access to sunlight or was blown down by strong winds. The double-stem bonsai is often found in normal large trees. In bonsai, this is unusual, but not uncommon. There are many of these styles in a bonsai gallery, and you can expect to find this incredibly natural-looking tree for which the owner has done a lot of work. Both stems have different diameters that contribute to the crown of the bonsai. Some bonsai have designs that have much more than two stems, either separate or from a single main stem. These different types of bonsai are some of your well-known styles to discover. Numerous bonsai manufacturers are trying to make the style harder, while beginners are doing the same with a lot of work on their element.

THE BONSAI CALENDAR - WHAT TO DO AND WHEN TO GET THE BEST BONSAI TREES

Since bonsai plants are actually trees, they must be cared for according to the same natural cycle that a tree needs outdoors. For the healthiest bonsai plants, it is a good idea to follow a maintenance calendar.

January - The trees are mostly at rest. This month you don't have time to take care of your bonsai plants. Water your bonsai trees just enough so the soil doesn't dry out.

February - Now is the time to wire your bonsai tree to shape it. The cut should be made this month before the start of the growing season.

March - You need to think about repotting your bonsai plants. Make sure you have the right soil mix, a sufficient amount of pots and some good fertilizer. If your bonsai plant is less than five years old, you need to repot it. If your bonsai tree is between five and twenty years old, it should only be repotted every two years. If your bonsai is over twenty years old, you will repot every three years. If your bonsai is more than 100 years old, you should not repot it more than every four or five years.

April - Bonsai plants begin to trigger the spring growth of flowers, leaves, and new green needles. Make sure that the bonsai plant is appropriately watered and supplied with the correct amount of fertilizer at this vital time.

May - This is a season of healthy growth. Be sure to push back the trailing leaves to ensure that the increase is bushy and full where you want it. A good irrigation schedule, especially in the evening, is now essential.

June - It is now safe to trim deciduous trees if necessary.

Keep pinching off unwanted shoots.

July - Temperatures rise. Good irrigation is just as important as protecting plants with delicate leaves from the scorching sun. For bonsai plants like maple or beech, it is best to protect them from direct sunlight and only leave the full sun in the morning and evening.

August - Keep your bonsai trees safe from the harsh sun. Lower the amount of nitrogen in your fertilizer mix as the strong growing season comes to an end.

September - Check all wired branches to make sure the bonsai plants have not grown enough to be pinched by the wires. Continue irrigation schedule.

October - Deciduous trees now show their colors and say goodbye to the growing season. This is an excellent time to trim heavier branches. You no longer have to water the bonsai trees that often.

November - Deciduous trees have now lost all leaves. If you keep your bonsai plants outside, now is the time to take them indoors.

December - At the end of the year, you should protect

your bonsai plants from too much cold. However, make sure that you don't place them close to a heat source. A bonsai plant is just that - a tree! You need a cold to stimulate the cycle of life.

Bonsai trees have something indefinable. Her exquisite beauty in miniature form, the way it puts you in a different perspective, the calmness that you feel when you just look at your tree is something that needs to be experienced rather than described. With bonsai trees in your home, you can be transported to another place, away from the hustle and bustle of modern life to a place of inner peace and serenity even more so once you have cared for and shaped these bonsai trees! Spending time with a bonsai plant, caring for it, shaping it, feeding it, and watering it means gradually entering into a kind of meditation. The world is closed as you study the shape of the tree, visualize the shape you want to lure your tree into, and plan the small steps required to achieve your goals. There is a lot to learn; there is a lot to practice ... but the payoff is invaluable. If you have achieved a few small successes with your bonsai, you run the risk of becoming addicted! But then what! There are far substandard things in this world that are addictive than the harmless and beautiful world of bonsai trees. Of course, nothing is really good without time and care. But the special thing about bonsai is that the path to perfection is an addiction! It is doing, not receiving, that soothes the mind. That's the whole point. However, before you can get lost in this type of meditation, you need to learn some basic skills.

Choose the type of bonsai trees you want to grow and equip yourself with some high-quality bonsai products. Spend some time getting the basics right, and you will have a lifelong interest in bonsai trees that will bring you tremendous satisfaction and joy.

HOW TO SELECT THE RIGHT PLACEMENT FOR YOUR BONSAI TREE

F IRST, YOU NEED TO find a suitable place for your bonsai tree. Choose a location that maintains a constant temperature. A bright and airy position without drafts is best. Most bonsai trees like some sunlight a few hours a day, but make sure your tree isn't exposed to direct sunlight for too long. Too much direct sunlight dries out the soil and roots too quickly. Insufficient water is the biggest killer of bonsai trees. So always remember how long your plant is exposed to direct sunlight. Have you ever had a favorite plant? Was it something that you germinated, planted, maintained, and successfully grew? There is nothing better than the feeling of finally seeing something sprout after weeks of tender care and patience. Bonsai trees are the perfect example of this process because your patient efforts reward you with a miniature version of an outdoor tree. When considering this type of plant, you must first consider the environment in which it will grow. Some of these trees are only indoors, while others prefer to be out of time. Some also enjoy full sunshine, while others thrive in mostly shady surroundings. This completely depends on the type of tree you selected. There is special soil for bonsai seeds, and you can also use plant foods as soon as they start growing. Most of these plants need to be watered daily, and they're usually not a really hardy plant. So once you've found a place where they're happy and growing well, it's probably best to allow them to stay there. As your bonsai tree grows, you'll learn how to shape and trim the branches. It is important to do this in the right way since either undercutting or overcutting creates problems for your miniature system. As soon as wooden branches appear, you can also use special-shaped wire to shape the familiar shapes of these beloved trees. If you want to renovate some of the amazing and beautiful plants from the Orient, a bonsai tree is an excellent choice. With the right care and preservation, they can live happily for many years and be passed on from family member to family member. Familiarize yourself with the care that your particular choice requires, and efforts will bring results in the long run.

Bonsai trees are special and cannot be seen everywhere. When your friends and family see what you've grown, it's a testament to your patience and stability. These are the types of plants that show a lot of their owner's personality and can be a very charming introduction to your home or office. The placement of exotic plants and trees is critical to their overall development and long-term survival. It determines not only the general happiness of the plants but also the general attractiveness for the living space. You should only make the final choice of location after considering several other factors. If part of your house or garden gets too much sunlight, you can let the sun grow. Loving plants that provide shade. It is also important that the plants have enough space to spread. Competing plants should not be very close to each other. Dominant and invasive plants and trees should be placed away from delicate plants. You should also consider the final size the plant is expected to reach. In this way, you avoid that driveways or sidewalks are not only blocked for you but sometimes also for your neighbors.

The composition of the floor bed should be fairly simple and convenient. You can use either peat moss or clay to make up most of your mix. Since peat moss is highly acidic, always add ground limestone to maintain the pH of the soil. To increase ventilation and drainage, you can include pine bark or sand in the mix. Adding vermiculite to the soil increases water retention. In new plants, sparingly used granulate fertilizers can be cheap as starter feed. Bottomless plants are planted with liquid feed, and the addition of fertilizers is advisable to provide the nutrients the plant needs. South facing always has warmer temperatures and better lighting conditions over a longer period of time but can lead to very high temperatures in midsummer.

The easterly position gives off warmth in the early morning, which can be bad for trees with frost since the smaller branches can thaw, but the frozen root ball cannot give off moisture so that the branches can be lost. If trees are frozen, you need to pay attention to the early morning sun. West facing has the evening and long summer light. The north exposure can have low light conditions and lower temperatures, which allows the trees to remain calm on warmer winter days. Care should be taken when positioning trees indoors. Locations above radiators and in full sun windows can create very dry conditions, and trees can have problems handling them. These are fairly tree-specific, but can essentially be divided into two main groups - hardy and not hardy, or tropical and subtropical, which are roughly the same class as trees, both outdoors and indoors. Indoor trees benefit from periods outside in warm weather, but be careful not to be damaged by cold nights. Outdoor trees struggle inside as they often find it too dry. In winter, keeping a deciduous tree in the foliage by taking it indoors can be very harmful. The occasional mild frost is often harmless for trees outdoors. Prolonged and heavy weather can lead to the death of small branches or the complete loss of trees.

You will have difficulty watering a compacted root ball effectively, and the roots can develop diseases and root rot due to the absence of oxygen. Bonsai are kept in their unique style by trimming them without tying a pot. After a short search, you will find endless information about bonsai care for every bonsai tree. Getting involved in the subtleties is one of the attractions of this popular hobby, but a healthy bonsai requires that you only follow a few basic principles. Healthy soil makes a healthy plant. Therefore, you should also pay special attention to the floor. Use a high-quality fertilizer and fungicide to extend the life of your plants. Important reminder: only a mild fungicide should be used. Dilute it in water before applying it to the floor. Improve your cutting skills.

CONCLUSION

WHETHER IT'S A BIRTHDAY, Secretary's Day, Mother's Day, Father's Day or the holidays (Christmas, Hanukkah or Kwanzaa), bonsai trees

are great gifts. Bonsai trees are a faultless gift for any loved one born with or without a green thumb. If you know someone who loves plant care and enjoys it, bonsai trees are indeed the perfect gift. Here you will find the items you need if you want to give a bonsai tree as a gift. First, you need to buy is a bonsai tree. Before you buy a bonsai tree, you need to determine whether your recipient needs an indoor or outdoor bonsai tree. Does the beneficiary live in a warm area or in an area where the seasons change? Next, you need to determine which types of bonsai trees you want to buy. There are many types of bonsai trees, such as Japanese maple, elm, ficus, maple, and juniper. Some bonsai tree genus is more difficult to grow than others, so you need to make sure that you choose the convenient species for the person who will receive the bonsai tree. The second thing you need to a bonsai pot. Nowadays, there are different styles, colors, shapes, and sizes to choose from, so you can easily find a bonsai pot for the bonsai tree that is perfect for everyone. When choosing the bonsai pot, you need to choose the right size for the bonsai tree to ensure that the tree fixes into the pot.

The third thing you need to buy is bonsai soil. Unlike other types of plants, bonsai trees need a certain type of soil to grow. Some floors are already fertilized to make your life easier. However, when you buy bonsai soil, you need to make sure that not only are you buying enough soil to fill the pot, you also need to add extra soil. The fourth thing you need to buy is bonsai fertilizer. Bonsai trees need fertilizer for growth and nutrition. There are many varieties to choose from, starting with organic and non-organic types. Regardless of which fertilizer you choose, you need to know what nitrogen content your bonsai tree needs. For safety's sake, buy additional fertilizer and pack it with your bonsai gift. The fifth thing you need to buy is wire and tools. These articles are indispensable, especially for beginners in bonsai cultivation. Bonsai tool sets are available and are supplied with standard tools such as bending lifters, concave cutters, scissors, and wire cutters. The wire is also important because the wire is used to shape the bonsai tree. The last thing you need to buy is a watering can or a watering can. Like most plants, bonsai trees need frequent watering. A watering can is a must as this subtly reminds you that the bonsai tree needs water.

Winter, spring, summer, or autumn: when it comes to bonsai trees can be a good time to buy a bonsai gift at any time. When giving away a bonsai tree, be sure to include a pot, soil, bonsai fertilizer, wire tools, and a watering kettle. By including these items, your bonsai gift will be the perfect gift! Another aesthetic principle of bonsai growth is the overall triangular shape for the visual balance and the representation of truth, goodness, and beauty. Trees are developed and cared for in a small container to slow their growth, and they are a cut miniaturized version of the real trees. It is possible to cultivate any trees. Bonsai trees are allowed to root in their containers on purpose, and the roots are also pruned. But root-bound plants won't thrive forever in this state, and bonsai trees need to be repotted every two or three years to give the roots new soil. Bonsai trees are really an art form. They are plants that are grown in bowls or containers and developed so that they stay small. Bonsai farmers in their childhood give bonsai trees much more attention. The main goal of the bonsai tree owner or bonsai tree builder is to create all the conditions under which the bonsai tree can grow strong, healthy, and aesthetically.

LISTEN TO THE AUDIOBOOK FOR FREE

DID YOU KNOW YOU CAN DOWNLOAD THE AUDIOBOOK VERSION OF THIS BOOK FOR FREE?

- VISIT **BIT.LY/BONSAI-US** FOR AUDIBLE US
- VISIT **BIT.LY/BONSAI-UK** FOR AUDIBLE UK

Made in the USA
San Bernardino, CA
18 July 2020

75695011R00075